Saul Steinberg

Hi Claire

SAUL STEINBERG

BY HAROLD ROSENBERG

ALFRED A. KNOPF IN ASSOCIATION WITH THE WHITNEY MUSEUM OF AMERICAN ART, NEW YORK, 1978

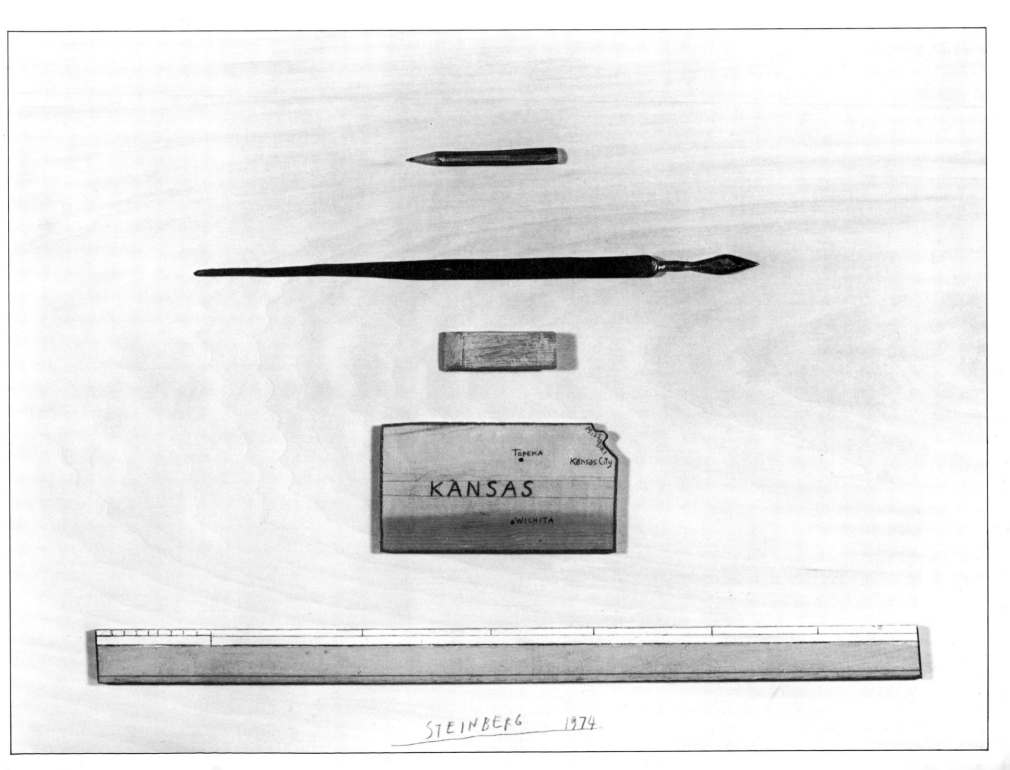

STEINBERG 1974

THIS IS A BORZOI BOOK PUBLISHED BY ALFRED A. KNOPF, INC.

Text © 1978 by the Whitney Museum of American Art.
Illustrations © 1942 to 1950 inclusive (renewed 1969 to 1977 inclusive) by Saul Steinberg.
Illustrations © 1951 to 1978 inclusive by Saul Steinberg.
Chronology © 1978 by Saul Steinberg.

All rights reserved under International and Pan-American Copyright Conventions.
Published in the United States by Alfred A. Knopf, Inc., New York, and
simultaneously in Canada by Random House of Canada Limited, Toronto.
Distributed by Random House, Inc., New York.

A John L. Hochmann Book

Of the 274 illustrations, 38 appeared previously in *The New Yorker;*
7 appeared in *Le Masque*, Maeght Editeur, Paris; 4 appeared
originally in *Flair* magazine © 1950 Cowles Magazines, Inc.;
6 appeared in *The Inspector,* Viking Press, New York.

Library of Congress Cataloging in Publication Data

Rosenberg, Harold.   Saul Steinberg.   Bibliography: p.
1. Steinberg, Saul. I. Whitney Museum of
American Art.
N6537.S7R67 1978   760′.092′4   77-20349
ISBN 0-394-50136-5
ISBN 0-394-73591-9 pbk.

Manufactured in the United States of America

First Edition

This book was published in conjunction with a major exhibition organized
by the Whitney Museum of American Art with the following travel itinerary:
Whitney Museum of American Art, New York, April 14–July 9, 1978;
Hirshhorn Museum and Sculpture Garden,
Smithsonian Institution, Washington, D.C.,
October 13–November 26, 1978; Arts Council of Great Britain,
Serpentine Gallery, London, January 17–February 25, 1979;
Fondation Maeght, Saint-Paul, France, March 15–April 30, 1979.

The exhibition was sponsored by SCM Corporation.
Tom Armstrong, Director of the Whitney Museum, served
as Director of the Exhibition, Harold Rosenberg as Guest Curator,
Jennifer Russell as Assistant Curator.

Photographs by Geoffrey Clements, and Henri Cartier-
Bresson, Robert Doisneau, Louis Faurer, Bruce Jones,
Eugene L. Mantie, Inge Morath, O. E. Nelson, Eric
Pollitzer, Nathan Rabin, John Schiff, Bill Strehorn,
Ken Strothman, Frank J. Thomas.

Contents

Albuquerque Academy

Sponsor's Foreword

It is more than a happy circumstance that the first American
retrospective of the work of Saul Steinberg takes place at the
Whitney Museum of American Art; it is most appropriate.
Although his uniquely American work has been displayed in
galleries and museums in the United States, the Whitney's
exhibition and book are the most comprehensive ever produced.
Perhaps because Steinberg is so well known through
his humorous drawings published in *The New Yorker*, too few
people are aware of the wide range and complexity of his work.
A draftsman whose formidable imagination is reflected in
both content and technique, Steinberg describes himself,
characteristically, as "a writer who draws." While many will see
the exhibition at the Whitney Museum and enjoy this book,
thousands more will view Steinberg's works as the exhibition
travels in this country and in Europe. We at SCM Corporation
are delighted to be able to join with the Whitney Museum
in celebrating the accomplishments of this major figure
in American art.

Paul H. Eliker, President
SCM Corporation

Director's Foreword

Presenting an exhibition and associated book about the work of Saul Steinberg is an activity that initially seems as redundant as introducing someone to his kinfolk. Everyone seems to recognize his work, and yet do we know the motivations and meanings underlying the images of this comic and mysterious adventurer? This is a basic theme in Harold Rosenberg's illuminating essay about Steinberg, in which he writes, "His art is the public disclosure of a man determined to keep his life a secret."

This is the first retrospective view of the work of an artist who has become internationally known through his published cartoons and drawings. Steinberg was reluctant about such a project because he did not want to witness the revelation of himself to the public. After he and I talked and agreed that perhaps it was important to exhibit all aspects of his work together for the first time, he very generously devoted his attention to assisting us. We are grateful because he has ultimately given us the privilege of gaining a more intimate understanding of the accomplishments of an outstanding creative intellect.

Harold Rosenberg has known Steinberg for many years and has observed both the man and his work through frequent associations in the art world and at *The New Yorker*. When we decided to undertake this venture, no one was better informed and he was always generous with his knowledge and advice.

SCM has encouraged this project with enthusiasm and cooperation, expressing its admiration for the artist and its support of the Whitney Museum. We are indebted for its initial confidence in our proposal to join in this endeavor and its sustained efforts to present the most comprehensive publication and exhibition.

Jennifer Russell has assisted in all aspects of the exhibition and book and has successfully satisfied the demands of every detail. It would have been impossible to achieve our objectives without the help of so many generous lenders, who allowed us to publish and exhibit works by Steinberg that have become an important and beloved part of their visual worlds. It has been a pleasure to work with our colleagues at the other museums presenting this exhibition: Abram Lerner, Cynthia McCabe and Howard Fox at the Hirshhorn Museum; Joanna Drew and Catherine Lampert at the Arts Council of Great Britain.

We are grateful to Paul Anbinder and the staff of Alfred A. Knopf for their cooperation in publishing this book. Daryl Harnisch and Jock Truman were extremely helpful in locating important works. Others who have assisted us include: Ernst Beyeler, Vivian Cavalieri, Jacques Dupin, Anita Duquette, Mrs. Stephen Halsey, Patricia Hobbs, John L. Hochmann, Sidney Janis, Lisa Ludwig, Claudia Neugebauer, Joan Ohrstrom, Betty Parsons, Peter Rathbone, Judith Richardson-Silvia, Linda Silverman, Mary Anne Staniszewski, Mrs. Helen Stark, Daniel Varenne, Michèle Venard.

To all the lenders, to the sponsor and especially to the artist, we extend the appreciation of a grateful public.

Tom Armstrong
Director

Saul Steinberg

aul Steinberg is a frontiersman of genres, an artist who cannot be confined to a category. He is a writer of pictures, an architect of speech and sounds, a draftsman of philosophical reflections. His line of a master penman and calligrapher, aesthetically delectable in itself, is also the line of an illusionist formulating riddles and jokes about appearances. In addition, it is a "line" in the sense of organized gab. Because he is attracted to pen and ink and pencils, and because of the complex intellectual nature of his products, one may think of Steinberg as a kind of writer, though there is only one of his kind. He has worked out exchanges between the verbal and the visual, including puns on multiple planes of verbal and visual meaning, that have caused him to be compared to James Joyce. His art-monologues bring into being pictures that are words, and words that have the solidity of things, and that suffer the misfortunes of living creatures, as when HELP! is bitten in half by a crocodile[1] and in WHO DID IT? the WHO causes the DID to crush the I of the IT.[2]

Steinberg's compositions cross the borders between art and caricature, illustration, children's art, *art brut*, satire, while conveying reminiscences of styles from Greek and Oriental to Cubist and Constructivist. His work is notably of the present day, yet it has an aura of the old-fashioned. As a cartoonist, Steinberg tantalizes those who wish to separate

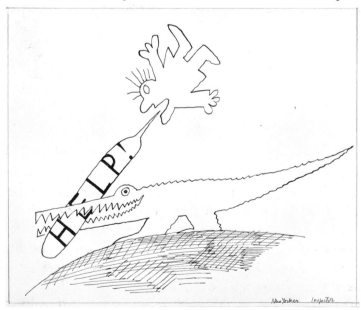

[1]*The vulnerable part of the man in danger is the cry for help, which is the part by which the crocodile holds him and which has the function of an appetizer. What do I want to say? That he who cries his terror becomes the victim of his statement. —S. St.*

[2]*It's obvious that* WHO *did it. And exactly the* H *of* WHO *shaped so as to push the* D *of* DID, *another word who obviously* did *it by its nature of* doing *and by the inclination of the two D's to roll and crush* IT; *more exactly, the* I *of* IT.

And who asks the question? None other than the Question Mark itself, facing and judging the fact. The three men are around for the sake of scale and animism. —S. St.

high art from the mass media. Granted that he is witty, formally ingenious, a great calligrapher, "Is he an artist?" Steinberg is aware that he is a borderline case, and seems content with the ambiguity of his position. "I don't quite belong in the art, cartoon or magazine world," he has reflected, "so the art world doesn't quite know how to place me." To display Steinberg's drawings and paintings in an art museum is, however, to define them as art. Since Marcel Duchamp showed a bicycle wheel in an art gallery more than fifty years ago, objects have been identified by the company they keep. By this rule, the present retrospective closes the debate about the works contained in it — but it will not determine the nature of a Steinberg reproduced in a magazine next week. Art today, cartoon tomorrow.

More important, however, than the obsolescent issue of "Is it art?" is the fact that all of Steinberg's creations form a single continuous and developing whole; that they are coherent with one another through the unique cast of this artist's thinking, skill and sensibility. It is this ultimate mental/manual signature that has brought Steinberg recognition as a master with a wider public throughout the world than any other artist now alive.

The tradition of the artist is to become someone else.
—SAUL STEINBERG

teinberg emerged among the American artists who in the immediate postwar years revolutionized painting and sculpture by introducing into it a new subject matter: the mystery of individual identity. "The self, terrible and constant, is for me the subject matter of painting," wrote Barnett Newman. Self or not-self (impersonality) has been the issue on which art movements in the United States have risen and foundered in the decades since the war. In their mythic researches, Arshile Gorky, Jackson Pollock, Willem de Kooning, Philip Guston, Barnett Newman, Mark Rothko each sought a unique idiom in which to unveil a being underlying consciousness.

Like them, Steinberg conceived art as autobiography. But autobiography of whom? The hidden metaphysical self. Man today? The immigrant? The stranger? In the mid-twentieth century the artist is obliged to invent the self who will paint his pictures — and who may constitute their subject matter.

Steinberg's approach to the self has been the opposite of the Expressionists'. It has also distinguished itself from that of the "impersonalists," such as Ad Reinhardt, Frank Stella, Donald Judd, and other minimalists. Instead of seeking

"contact" (Pollock's term) with the singular, unattainable self, Steinberg conceived the theater of Abstract Man, Mr. Anybody (and his wife), in their countless poses, self-disguises and self-creations. Each of the women in *Bingo in Venice, California,* for example, is an invention produced by collaboration between herself and the artist's pen (page 42).

A virtuoso of exchanges of identity, Steinberg is naturally inclined toward comedy. His concept of the comic relates both to the fantasies of human beings and to their rigidities. Comedy also arises out of his consciousness of self-invention. Steinberg's art is a parade of fictitious personages, geometric shapes, items of household equipment, personified furniture, each staged in a fiction of what it is—or in a dream of being something else. His little man, anonymous citizen, is burdened with projects and conditions, from sneaking up on a question mark with a butterfly net to dreaming of a woman who is dreaming of him. A roughly

drawn, freehand cube has a dream of glory in which it is a perfected cube with ruled edges and neatly lettered corners (*Cube's Dream,* page 12). An E built of massive blocks fancies itself as an elegant French *É* (page 61). In Steinberg's view everything that exists is an artist and is engaged in refining its appearance—a curious version of Darwinism. "The main thing to find out," he declared to an interviewer, "is what sort of technique the crocodile employs to show itself."

There is also a grim side to this universal self-transformation. Becoming someone else is a crisis situation. Steinberg's drawings are full of figures on the edges of precipices, statues falling from their pedestals, solitary individuals staring into voids.

In contrast to the impenetrable but suggestive signs evoked by Pollock and de Kooning from the spontaneous action of the brush, Steinberg's figurative language, equally mysterious, derives from the gallery of images firmly fixed in the

11

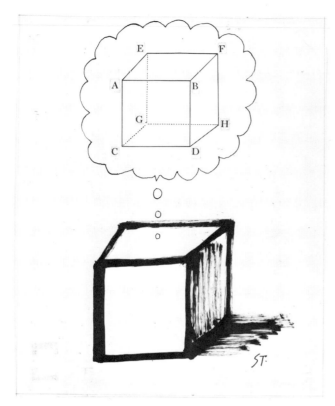

public mind. In this respect, as in others we shall discuss later, Steinberg is a forerunner of Pop Art—though he transcends the limits of Pop, since he is above all an artist of the free imagination. From the faked official signatures and governmental seals in his drawings of the 1940s to the rubber stamps of his 1970s paintings and assemblages, he has been telling his story in terms of impersonal and repeatable commonplaces, distorted, as in dreams, by exaggerations, displacements and wit. Impresario of Abstract Man, he stages him in a universe of accepted ideas that he suddenly strips of their acceptance; for example, his use of Uncle Sam. It is not surprising that a specialist in the riddles of identity—is this what the Sphinx stands for in Steinberg's recent paintings?—should be aware that autobiography is a species of fiction writing. Those who strive to lay bare the "facts" of their lives are victims of the delusions of the style called Realism. Steinberg's presence in his visual narrative is personified by a cast of invented characters who serve as his disguises: the little man in profile (the citizen, more or less Solid), the cat (the little man with a tail and whiskers), the dog (a more dignified cat), the fish (Sphinx to the cat), the artist (the hand with the pen, the little man with an easel), the hero (a knight on horseback). These personae perform in varieties of domestic and comic-strip situations, from watching TV and scrutinizing pictures in art galleries to marching in formation on mathematical moonscapes. Instead of presenting himself as protagonist, Steinberg projects an alter ego who is detached, curious, passive and fearful—one of his

most memorable trademarks is the gentleman inside of whose head is a rabbit peering out of the man's eyes, a frightened creature, both trapped and protected (*The Rabbit*). Accessible only through his metaphors, Steinberg becomes "someone" in his demonstrations of how his anonymous inner being is constantly re-presenting itself.

To investigate individual identity in terms of its social reality is to function in the realm of farce. Comedy is what makes Steinberg immediately attractive, and it is the basis of his popularity. His narrative art looks back to Molière, at the same time that it takes its place with the absurdist literature of this century. The restrictions of the line drawing have not prevented Steinberg from being the peer of Pirandello, Beckett, Ionesco. To a style founded on the drawings of children, he has added the dimension of playful juggling with the gravest issues of art and self.

The artist tells his story of "becoming someone else" through pictures that suggest possibilities rather than recount facts. In *Hotel Plaka*, two conversational balloons are erotically intertwined on a bed covered with a massive comforter.[3] Steinberg narrates but he does not reveal: in the Hotel Plaka bedroom two voices met; that's all you'll ever know. Steinberg has said that at the age of ten he decided to become a novelist but that he has still not made up his mind about what to be. The advantage of being a borderline artist is that it allows the decision to be put off indefinitely. With his name multiplied in every big-city telephone book, Steinberg can come close to anonymity without effort. In an apartment house in New York where Steinberg lived, there were two Steinbergs on the same floor—and in East Hampton where he has a house there is another Saul Steinberg. The absence of an identity of one's own can

become oppressive, as Willie Sutton discovered when he lived incognito in Brooklyn. A few years ago, Steinberg lost his patience and telephoned his East Hampton namesake.

"Is this Saul Steinberg?" he inquired.

"Yes" was the answer.

"But are you the *real* Saul Steinberg?"

"No," replied the poor fellow.

"Are you sure?"

Yet, knowing and not knowing who he is, the artist can "express himself" as if he were somebody. In his drawings Steinberg records everything about himself but without providing information—except what he has been making up. His art is the public disclosure of a man determined to keep his life a secret.

Steinberg's adventures in disguise begin with his birth in Romania, which he has dubbed "a masquerade country." The moment he opened his eyes he was convinced that his operetta environment, with its costumed peasants and mustachioed cavalrymen, was calculated to trick him. His defense was to learn without delay how to render himself invisible by blending into his surroundings. But Romania was ready for him: "At school I had a military uniform and a number like a license plate, so anybody could take my number and denounce me."

At eighteen, Steinberg left for Italy, a country not without its own operatic delusions, especially during the reign of Mussolini, when businessmen paraded after hours in black shirts and spurred boots and Il Duce harangued mobs from

---

[3]*Hotel Plaka, a hotel in Athens. This is part of a series of erotic drawings—a parody of pornography, showing how conventionally we are exploited by eroticism. Here the eroticism is represented only by the location: a bedroom in a hotel, the most banal setting for eroticism. Love here is a dialogue in bed; two balloons merge. In another drawing, a Cubist element is in bed with the Impressionist technique, and here is another one again where a Pythagorean triangle transfixes a question mark. One could say that the question mark, fat and voluptuous, is the woman, while the triangle, precise, geometric, the symbol of logic, is the man. But this exposes our prejudices, because one thinks always of the man as the logical part, while the woman is a simple question mark with all the insecurity implicit in this symbol. It could be in fact an affair between a fat man and a smart woman. In other drawings, I put in bed certain numbers that are erotic because of their construction: 5 and 2, for instance (1, 4 and 7 have no sex appeal). —S. St.*

balconies. For the next six years, dividing his time between studying architecture (reflected in the ornate bridges and railroad stations [page 43], fairy-tale castles, period-design skyscrapers [page 89], stylized interiors, Utopian city layouts and ornamental cloud formations that provide exotic elements in his drawings) and making cartoons for Milanese periodicals, he adopted the look—spectacles, long hair and bushy mustache—of the typical professional-school student.

Mussolini's partnership with Hitler and the spread of the war forced Steinberg to seek a new setting, and with it a change of costume. The place for him, obviously, was the United States, a land where everyone is busily engaged in becoming someone else—thus, in Steinberg's terms, an artist. To reach this Promised Land was not easy in wartime. Steinberg arrived in Lisbon with a "slightly fake" passport—one that had run out but that he resuscitated by means of forged rubber stamps. (Steinberg's studio today stocks enough rubber stamps to get him safely around the entire cosmos.) At the airport Steinberg was arrested, not on account of the passport but through a mistake of identity (another Steinberg or someone who resembled him physically was wanted) and because he infuriated the Portuguese police by denying that he spoke Portuguese, which they took as an insulting pretense. Shipped back to Italy, he managed, after some painful experiences about which he prefers to remain silent, to make his way to the Dominican Republic, where he emerged as a colonial gentleman, planter style, in a white linen suit and a broad-brimmed panama.

Admitted to the United States—in contrast to Romania a nation of civilians—Steinberg found himself once again in uniform, this time the outfit of a naval officer. Now masquerading professionally, and in deadly earnest, he was sent to China by the Navy as a "weather observer." His actual mission was to act as a means of communication with the Chinese guerrillas by means of his ability to say things through pictures. The hitch, Steinberg insists, was that while he and the Chinese understood each other perfectly, he could not communicate with the Americans since he knew no English. His theory is that his real mission was to confuse enemy intelligence agents by compelling them to wonder what this foreigner was doing with the United States Navy in China. The fiction within fictions of the intelligence service made Steinberg feel at home.

To wear a uniform and be an alien underneath is to experience style as disguise. For Steinberg, place is dress (e.g., *Moscow Winter Coats*, opposite, bottom right) and dress is playacting. Every self-affirmation is a masquerade. The world is a Romania. The West is the Wild West of *High Noon*, sombreros and cartridge belts, hand on the pistol, the Fastest Gun. The cowboy appurtenances form a design—the barroom boaster is a piece of architecture, his legs arched like a bridge (page 40). Steinberg's succession of uniforms sharpened his conviction that the style hides the man. Not only the artist but everyone "becomes someone else" in becoming someone. One is thought about, thus invented. Or, as Steinberg put it with memorable succinctness in his *Cogito* drawings (page 12): "I think, therefore Descartes is." One creates not oneself but another. Being is in the act. A drawing of women is called *Four Techniques*, as if the existence of each were someone's "how to." Another drawing carries the idea further: in *Techniques at a Party* seventeen different styles of drawing have replaced the human substance of a crowd.

In America masks are worn less tightly than in Europe, where they are affixed permanently by class and vocation— "in order," says Steinberg, "to make the job of tax collecting easier." In America it is even chic to shift periodically to the mask of anonymity, providing it is transparent and can be seen through by everyone. Thus professors and poets jitterbug to pass as common folk, tycoons address each other as "Joe" and "Frank" and Presidents are headlined in monograms as FDR and LBJ. Conversely, people whom nobody knows disguise themselves in dark glasses in order to pretend to be incognito—that is, someone who is making an effort to remain unknown. Individuals unmasking themselves only to reveal other masks, verbal clichés masquerading as things, a countryside that is an amalgam of all imported styles (*Rainbow Landscape*, page 140), an outlook that is at once conventional and futuristic—America was made to order for Steinberg. In the nation of "The Man That Was Used Up," as the title of Poe's tale put it, Steinberg's life of ruses and disguises could fulfill itself.

Steinberg's own mask after becoming an American was one of imperturbable curiosity, that of a species of unofficial inspector (*The Inspector* is the title of one of his published collections of drawings), most approximately an inspector of insect life, a mask which in time was divested of its mustache and most of its hair but on which still glitter the old student's eyeglasses. What chiefly occupied the attention of this investigator was the remarkable capacity of his fellow citizens to contrive selves without limit in an environment that was the projection of what each desired to be at the moment (opposite, bottom left). His observations gave rise to the series of drawings in which a man or a cat draws a line that outlines his own shape and frames him in a scene (*The Spiral*, page 16).

15

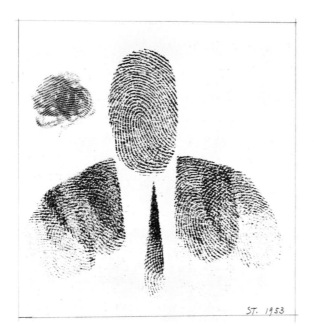

Among the American artists who after the war made the experience of self-creation central to their work, the majority—Gorky, de Kooning, Hofmann, Rothko, Gottlieb, Newman, Guston, Baziotes—were immigrants or sons of immigrants. This aspect of their situation has rarely been mentioned, much less analyzed in relation to their creations. With Steinberg, his condition of being an immigrant affects his work to a degree that cannot be overlooked. With the immigrant, the issue of "Who am I? What shall I become?" is sharpened by "Where am I?" All the artist identity-seekers have been painters of mythical landscapes. With them, figure and setting, self and nature-symbol are one. Self-creation and man-created nature go hand in hand. In de Kooning's "Woman" canvases, the human torso loses its contours and dissolves into fields and bodies of water. Gorky entitles an abstract landscape *How My Mother's Apron Unfolds in My Life.* Hofmann testifies that "I bring the landscape home in me," while Gottlieb invents signs that indicate new solar bodies on his cosmic maps. Steinberg's America, with its distorted distances, Uncle Sams, eagles, Masonic pyramids, Last of the Mohicans, matrons, hookers, crocodiles and cats, though made up of fact and popular legend, is no less the projection of an estranged self than Rothko's floating plateaus of tint.

Steinberg may be said to have begun discovering Steinberg America in the Immigration Office. Official documents are among the most stylized elements in modern society. Passports, drivers' licenses, bonding stamps, ID cards change very little. Also tax receipts, protocols, birth certificates, citizenship papers. The rubber stamp hovers over society's business as did formerly the king's seal. Diplomas, proclamations, bank drafts are signed and countersigned.

All these are affirmations of form—that is, art as the antidote of anarchy. People also leave formal traces of themselves in doodles, laundry tickets, albums.

Steinberg noted that a fingerprint has the oval shape of the human face; outfitting this unfailing mark of individual identity with a collar and tie also made of fingerprints provided an improved version of a passport photo (*Passport Photo*). A fingerprint photo is an abstraction, yet it is the essence of a portrait. It doesn't resemble the sitter but it is his organic signature. To emphasize the point, Steinberg accompanied fingerprint portraits with parodies of conventional album pictures (page 66). The concrete representation fades, the abstraction holds firm.

In another drawing, the fingerprint portrait, affixed to a legal-looking document complete with counterfeit official seals, stamps, watermarks and ornate signatures, provides a certificate of status. The immigrant is now legally "here," though his proof of identity is forged. Or, one might say, the artist's pen has taken over the function of government, as it has the molding of nature and its inhabitants. Steinberg's fake government instruments, self-generated global identification papers, are his equivalent of Gorky's self-documentation in *The Artist and His Mother,* based on an old flashbulb photo.

But Steinberg was not finished with the fingerprint. There are drawings in which the texture of the finger ends constitutes the substance of the heavens (*Fingerprint Landscape*). The artist is encompassed by the physical sign of his identity in the same way—and with the same implication of a world emanating from self—as he is in the circle that the little man draws and stands on and that closes him in. The fingerprint and the pen are equally the sources of this newcomer artist's universe. Finally there is a drawing of the artist painting a landscape with a bunching of fingerprints at the horizon that produces a lowering mood like the cypresses of van Gogh. With his rhetoric of signs, Steinberg melds self and surroundings into an ego/cosmos as explicit as that of Rothko and Pollock.

The immigrant digs in where he can obtain security. Gorky, de Kooning, Newman, Rothko settled in New York City, Connecticut, Long Island, places from which they explored their environments of projected self. In contrast, Steinberg arrived in New York only to keep moving. Being an immigrant was a condition that he apparently preferred and that has taken him a long time to overcome. That fingerprint self-portrait had perhaps a deeper meaning than he realized. To keep arriving and identifying himself are, it would seem, among his deepest impulses, and the places from which he has departed supply him with rich veins of nostalgia—the lonely goodbyes in his travel "postcards," bearing names such as *Abidjan* and *2 Eastern Sunsets* (pages 146 and 147).

"By putting oneself in the uncomfortable position of the immigrant, one is again like a child." But a child of oceanic or global sensibility. Marc Chagall paints the *shtetl* of his White Russian childhood, Gorky his fabulous Armenia. Steinberg's art lacks a centrifugal location. His nostalgia, fabricated of yesterdays, is skin deep.

For Steinberg, as for his Abstract Expressionist contemporaries, the landscape is an emanation of the artist. There are Steinbergs with skies made of rhythmically repeated pen strokes, zigzags and scribbles, fields composed of parallel horizontal lines, ornamental patterns, script—as arbitrary as Pollock's wavy strands of paint. Even the horizon is not immune to molestation: in a 1962 Steinberg it curls up into an erratic S producing two landscapes (two universes) joined in different eye levels, with a void between them.

But Steinberg's invented landscapes are not totally subjective or metaphysical. Here again his position is on the boundary line—between the self and the not-self, between the internal and the factual. He is a reporter of fictions, as well as an originator of them. His story of himself includes the record of his travels. His pen has journeyed from Milan to Greenwich Village, to Colorado and Hollywood, to Zurich, Moscow, Samarkand, Murchison Falls—to a prison city called *Law and Order* (page 152), to a pitted terrain that could be the moon. His mythical landscapes are also the settings of collective myths, scenes and cities fabricated by the dreams of their inhabitants. In his fantasy of America are embedded fragments of popular symbols, the romance of frontier history and the bad taste of automobile designers, Hollywood architects, fashion experts and dog groomers.

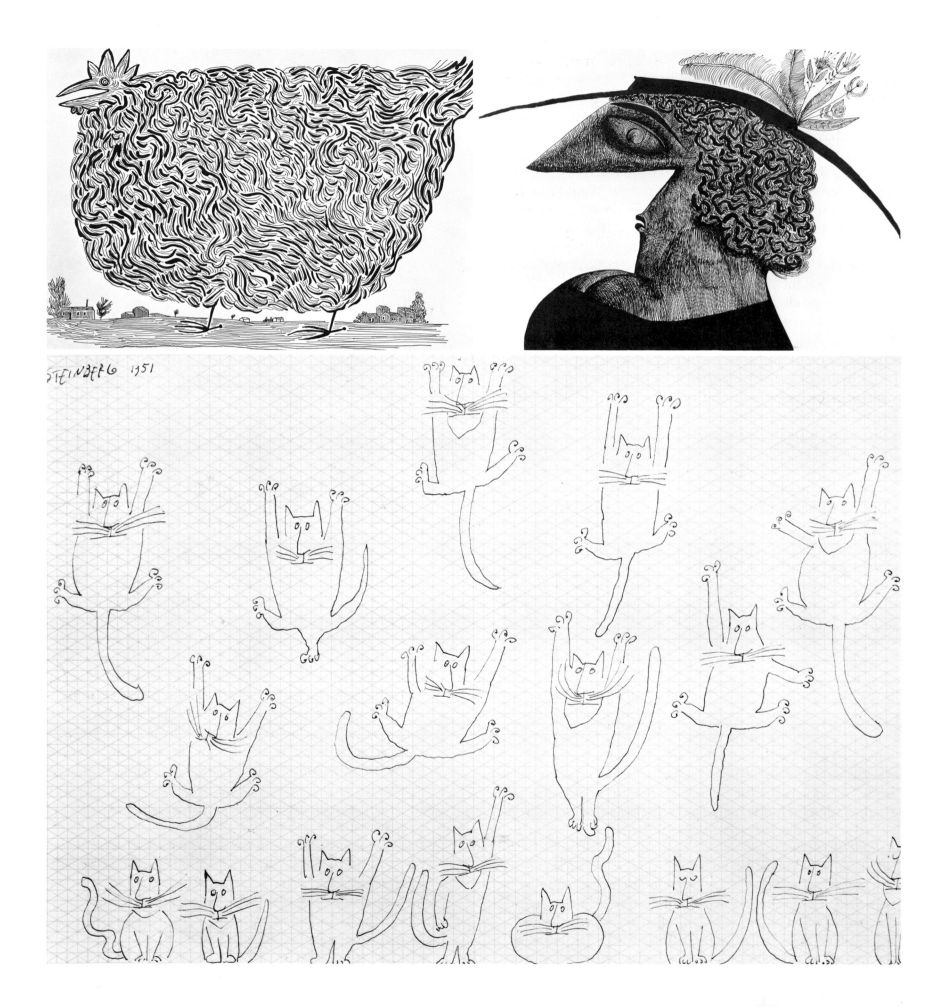

The theme of a world unfolding out of the artist's act of drawing is reiterated in numerous ways, from the calligraphic landscape mentioned above, in which the horizon explodes into a flourish of penmanship, to drawings in which objects are repeated upside down because a line indicates a body of water in which they are reflected. To Steinberg the line of the horizon, which marks the limit of the visible, is just another line that his pen can manipulate as it sees fit. All things in Steinberg's pictures—scenes, people, cats, crocodiles—have their source in art. But art is not restricted to pictures. Everything that exists has its source in art; that is, in human invention. The skin on the fingertip is an organic product, but the fingerprint is a device of society. It is a mark produced with ink for the purpose of recording the identities of individuals and arranging them in files. The fingerprint is art imposed on nature by society.

Only objects as they are transformed by society's invention are proper subjects for Steinberg. Originating in an art-conceived universe, Steinberg's metaphorical images spread like varieties of mold throughout his compositions of the past thirty-five years, from the wartime cartoons and faux-naïve chickens and human heads (*Hen*, 1945, *Head*, 1945) shown in the Fourteen Americans exhibition of the Museum of Modern Art, New York, in 1946—and collected in *All in Line* (1945), with the self-originating hand holding a pen on its cover—to the most recent oil-on-paper landscapes and drawing-table assemblages. Analyzing the means by which things are commonly represented in art and out of it provides Steinberg with access to a Pandora's box of deceptive equivalents, as in his drawing of cats clinging to an imprisoning screen consisting of a sheet of graph paper on which the cats are drawn (*Graph Paper Cats*).

Steinberg himself has formulated his conception of nature as a human fabrication, a conception epitomized in his remark made several years ago: "When I admire a scene in the country, I look for a signature in the lower right-hand corner." Nature, in Steinberg's view, bears the imprint of the social and political world, including the forms provided by the accumulated styles of the past. "I can't draw a landscape," he has said, "but I draw man-made situations. . . . What I draw is drawing, [and] drawing derives from drawing. My line wants to remind constantly that it's made of ink."

Perhaps it is his conviction that his personae, buildings, animals can be dripped back into the ink bottle that gives Steinberg his lightness of touch, which eludes his scores of imitators. "Drawing derives from drawing" is the creed of the aesthete, and there is no doubt that there is much in Steinberg's drawing that is owing to the pure pleasure of

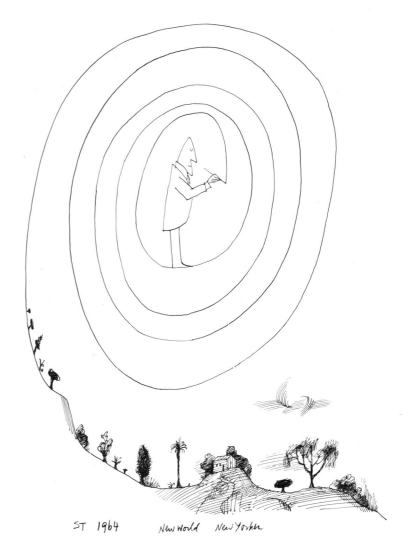

ST 1964   New World   New Yorker

execution. But Steinberg has no use for aestheticism. "To be involved in aesthetics only . . . ," he has said, "that for me is worthless. I want to say something." Beyond his aestheticism are his researches into self; and autobiography, whatever its form, is deadly serious. In Steinberg's compositions there is, besides drawing and what can come out of drawing, the grit of reality, of personal experience, at times painful.

Everything springs from the artist's act. The hand that makes the drawing has drawn itself and the pen with which it draws. In one complex Steinberg, the man with the pen has drawn a horizon, complete with trees, a road, a house, that has wound up into a spiral in the sky that he goes on drawing as it tightens around him (*Spiral*). "It gets narrower and narrower," Steinberg said. "This is a frightening drawing. It could be the life of the artist who lives by his own essence. He becomes the line itself and finally, when the spiral is closed, he becomes nature." One begins with fictions and converts them into realities through performance.

The material in Steinberg's art is neither things as they are nor the appearance of things, but the art in things, their style. Style is a disguise, but one that represents the history of the object and its social reality. It is the "imprint of the society and the political world" that makes people interesting to Steinberg. Steinberg finds these "imprints" everywhere: on the faces of living people, on places and objects, not merely in the comic books and advertising that inspired Pop artists. He ranges from wildly improbable coiffures, a face structured like a hat rack or flowing like rippling water, meditations of a dog, to Mickey Mouse strumpets that are all legs.

What we call "nature" is the sum of styles that coexist in any given period. The historical consciousness of modern times has provided the artist with a vastly expanded "politicized" nature in which to work. Like Joyce, Steinberg parodies styles spotted throughout history as potential costumes for the contemporary ego. The old platitude "Nature imitates art" has been raised to a higher intensity by the multiplication of styles, as well as by the physical superimposition upon the earth and its creatures of man-made contrivances. For Steinberg, anything that has escaped being made over by man fails as subject matter for art. "A beautiful woman is like a rainbow, a sunset, a moon—all stuff that should be looked at but not painted." Of course, Steinberg does paint rainbows, sunsets and moons and even, occasionally, a beautiful woman, because these, too, are "imprintings" of society in his sense. But he paints them as products of the techniques of painting. "Dogs and cats," he has explained, "are man made. I also draw lions. They entered society through allegory and coats of arms." At any rate, his point is clear: the matter of his art is artifice, the way people and things make themselves up, or are made up, to present themselves to the world. The more made up the better, since masquerade is evidence that the imagination has been at work. "I don't touch children much, except the sort of midgety ones that have been rendered political by being dressed in tiny Brooks Brothers suits."

In essence, art is, in Steinberg's term, a "political" activity; that is to say, conscious of the spectator as someone to affect, either as critic or as potential admirer and patron. Art is a response to the temptation to put on an act and to transform oneself—into an anonymous citizen, a cat, a movie star, a knight, a Sphinx. In the absence of the passion for playacting and social recognition, art is inconceivable. Thus art leads not toward reality but away from it, toward makeup, costume and role playing. Its highest gift is fame, on which Steinberg meditates in his numerous drawings of figures on pedestals. But fame, far from stabilizing the self, envelops it more completely in a maze of social abstractions. So the artist, too, is "man made," an object rather than a subject.

Nature not only imitates art, it imitates artists. After millennia of human image-making, it has gotten into the habit of showing off its versatility. Nature *arts*—people, animals, skies get themselves up to look like objects in pictures. Trees try to resemble trees; some (as in *Bird and Insects*, page 55) only manage to look like insects. In *Battle*, as in other Steinbergs, women resemble birds (page 56). Art birds, not real birds. Cats delude themselves into thinking they are cats—Steinberg says, "They think they are people." Yet with a few minor changes his *Giant Cat*, which resembles a work of American naïve art, could become a rhinoceros. Other cats are really coiled springs asleep in blue milk. Mountains ham the craggy look. Nature is engaged in improving its appearance under the direction of Darwin, or in dressing up for parts in *A Midsummer Night's Dream*. Steinberg's sensibility has a touch of the Shakespearian: personifying nature, he refers to a chipmunk as "he." Even a plant on his lawn is a character who somehow got the idea of appearing in green, being six inches tall and having petals for a face.

Nature is an artist and, like all artists, is ruled by clichés. Nature repeats itself, with and without variations, and in time the repeated image becomes an indelible sign. "For nature," says Steinberg, "and for whatever is untouched by people, I use a series of clichés." This is another way of saying that he replaces nature with residues of art.

The Rocky Mountains, lakes, cloud masses have been reiterated in pictures until they have become forms purged of content. Yet the earth and the creatures that inhabit it strive constantly for aesthetic effects—and succeed. When Steinberg came to America, he has said, it "amazed me to see old women dressed up in the most elaborate, sexy way. It took me some time to realize that this was a way to clown the situation of not being so young or beautiful any more; the way autumn clowns nature: red and yellow trees, dead leaves dancing and crossing the highway gaily." But while Steinberg employs clichés, he never uses them as is. Rather, he energizes the inert matter of the collective mind with his own imagination and endows it with the capacity for metamorphosis. In *Tuscarora Sphinx*, Steinberg's old friend Uncle Sam, with his Abe Lincoln stovepipe and chin beard, shows up transformed into a Sphinx sitting on guard before the pyramid on the backside of the one-dollar bill that represents the Novus Ordo Seclorum of the United States. In the drawing, the American eagle, also reduced to being an emblem on the back of the dollar, has managed to get off the ground and is reflected in a one-line lake, together with an Indian and a dog in a canoe, a swan, a side of the pyramid and two trees, only one of which appears on land. With a toy cannon at his side, Uncle Sam Sphinx is crouching in front of the pyramid of the New Order, defending it against a stick-figure Indian warrior on horseback armed with a lance

and carrying a curious device like a street lamp or an architectural ornament. The desert scene, with its sun or rainbow of concentric circles, impossibly continued in the depths of the lake, is as full of mysteries as Rousseau's *Sleeping Gypsy*, which, come to think of it, is also composed of remodeled clichés.

The strategy of the cliché is to escape notice. It is a form of statement, in words or in pictures, that through repetition achieves unscrutinized acceptance. How many Americans are aware, for example, that the dollar bill has a human eye on its backside and a pyramid that is a tribute to Freemasonry? The cliché replaces thought with the set phrase, and experience with the set image. It represents the parts of conversation we manage not to hear, the pictures on the wall we never see. Today, with the help of the media, the cliché is more effectively camouflaged than the contents of the lowest depths of the unconscious. Steinberg is as alert to clichés as a tax inspector to concealed income. Because he was an immigrant, what was commonplace to natives was an oddity to him; through persisting in reimmigrating, he has preserved his newcomer's astonishment. Rather than overlook repetitive images, he has been inclined to take them literally, like the rubber stamps with which he authenticates his landscapes. In the ubiquitous American emblems, he believes he has established contact with the bottommost layers of the American mind. His fellow with the high hat and scimitar-shaped whiskers, his American eagle with an E Pluribus Unum tape in its claws, his Statue of Liberty in a nightgown are as pungent figurations of the American past as the paintings of backwoods naïves or the sleigh scenes of Currier & Ives (*Sam's Troubles*, page 64). *Five Uncles* (page 21) is as captivating in the arbitrariness of its draftsmanship as Edward Hicks's *The Peaceable Kingdom*, with the added feature that it relates mythical America to the myths of the East by perching the Washington Monument on the back of a turtle.

Like a jungle witch doctor, Steinberg inhabits a universe of signifying signs, recondite yet immediately recognizable. On the other hand, he has produced drawings that cannot be fathomed even by himself. Though his work probably has a larger circulation than that by any other artist alive, his published pieces include some that are in fact impenetrable. Perhaps the explanation is that this artist on the borderline of genres also operates on the borderline of the consciousness of his time. "I appeal," he has said, "to the complicity of my reader ["reader" indicates the degree to which Steinberg thinks of himself as a writer rather than as a graphic artist], who will transform this line into meaning by using our common background of culture, history, poetry. Contemporaneity in this sense is a complicity." There is an echo here

Inge Morath, 1958

of the New Testament dictum "the children of this world are in their generation wiser than the children of light"—an esoteric tribute to the capacity of those living at the same time to comprehend by contiguity what they cannot grasp by reason.

Perceiving reality as the art in things is the root principle of Steinberg's aesthetics. This is another aspect of his work that relates it to Pop Art. By means of formal analogies, Pop succeeded in transmuting everyday objects and images (containers, ads, labels, comics) into paintings and sculptures in the museum tradition. Essentially, Pop is a continuation of the insight of Duchamp regarding the situation of art in an age of mechanical reproduction, when masterpieces compete with copies of themselves and manufactured products circulated on a mass basis, in which the *Mona Lisa* and a bicycle wheel are placed on the same aesthetic plane. Art is art because the museum can elevate common objects, including refashioned reproductions, into art by accepting them as such. Thus Pop artists have woven connections (e.g., Benday dots and the paint dots of Seurat) between comic strips, food containers, five-and-ten objects and art in museums. Yet the entire undertaking, from Duchamp onward, of converting aesthetic social substances into art through their likeness to physical features of works in the museum is essentially academic and frivolous. Pop Art begins and ends with objects to be admired as art on the basis of resemblances of the new work to the art of the past.

Reversing the practice of Duchamp, Steinberg surpasses the aestheticism of Pop Art. Instead of transferring usable objects into the museum, he siphons museum forms into his own popular art. In Steinberg's people-looking-at-art drawings, the spectators are more far-fetched stylistically than the pictures they are scrutinizing (page 96). In sum, Steinberg demonstrates that the art-making of life affects people and things before contemporary art gets to them. In its double derivation from art, Pop erects a superfluous barrier between fact and imagination, while Steinberg sees the imagination as the origin of the forms of facts.

In connection with a magazine interview of a decade ago,

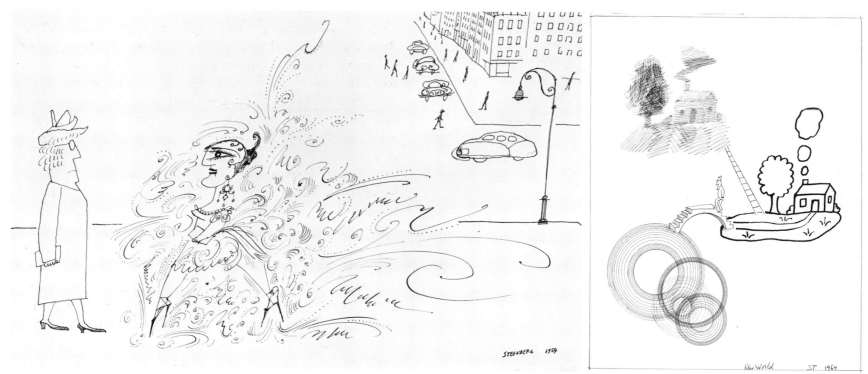

Steinberg is shown wearing a mask consisting of a drawing of his face on a paper bag. Once again, as in the fingerprint portraits, he had chosen to represent himself by means of an artifact produced by himself. Discussing his false face, he attributed it to a wish for the objectively lasting, as opposed to the constant metamorphosis of real things. He felt intimidated when a photographer pointed a camera at him. "So I made paper-bag masks of my face. I was able to relax inside the mask [the rabbit in the human head] and show a constant public image of myself to the camera." The mask, in a word, has the stability of a cliché, of the fixed idea. Steinberg says nothing about the expressiveness of which masks are capable, as in Japanese theater, for example. In this instance, he is merely thinking about the mask as a fabricated substitute that serves as a cover of the real face; it is not another self. But in *Two Dogs* (1975, page 212) the paper-bag faces have turned into savage grotesques; one is a female monster.

In the interview, Steinberg went on to say that it was gratifying to have the photographer take a photo not of Steinberg but of a drawing by him, "not reality but a symbol—a fantasy created by me.... Instead of catching that famous fleeting moment (which, photographers insist, reveals the essence of the sitter), that peculiar expression of my face, I gave them something steady that I made." However ephemeral drawings on grocery bags are, they transcend nature and time through the fact that they are made by man. In his discussion of the mask as self-portrait, Steinberg reverts to the antique version of the portrait as a simplified and abstracted summary of the subject's features, rather than the rendering of a visual impression of an actual face.

Nature differs from other artists in that it has no objection to mixing styles; it tolerates baroque clouds in the same scene with biomorphic lakes and mathematically layered cliffs. It is also prone to throwing in arbitrarily designed lakes or anatomies, forms that represent nothing but simply are. Steinberg's art identifies itself with the eclecticism of nature in his ability to absorb any style of picture-making that attracts his attention as distinct from the determination of most artists since the war to achieve singleness of form and effect. He objects neither to the juxtaposition of mutually exclusive modes nor to the merely impulsive. In a drawing in which "Sennelier" changes into "Steinberg," the artist seems to have let himself ride from association to association. A realistic drawing or a photo is as fully a mask as an abstract drawing, a cartoon or a fantasy, and Steinberg does not hesitate to use all these modes, and even to combine different ones in the same drawing. In compositions such as *Three Women*, he makes a point of posing modes of representation against one another (page 180). In *Waiting Room*, two male heads are shaped like daggers, exclamation points or Giacometti's elongated figures, and two children have the heads of cartoon animals (page 190). Bodies, with or without clothes, are also masks, as can be seen in Steinberg's drawings of torsos in bathtubs. Steinberg comes closest to imitating nature in the multiplicity of his devices. In this era of reductionist art, it is difficult to think of a motif—cities, deserts, railroad stations, hotel lobbies, words, industrial and military compounds, cafeterias, animals, people—that his idiom does not encompass.

The whole history of art influenced me: Egyptian paintings, latrine drawings, primitive and insane art, Seurat, children's drawings, embroidery, Paul Klee.

—SAUL STEINBERG

Together with the story of his life, Steinberg's ultimate subject matter is style—the forms that things, places, people have assumed through moods of nature and through human invention and copying. Style is used for psychological effect in *Bingo in Venice, California* (page 42), in which the faces of the old ladies in the foreground are composed of descending rows of dots, parallel lines, squiggles and feathers. *Two Cultures* (1954) makes its point through its title: two women are passing each other on the street; one is a staid Puritan matron of middle age, drawn in straight lines, the other a painted and bangled Carmen striding through the music of sprays of dots and curlicues. In *Techniques at a Party* (page 15), seventeen people consist entirely of the different manners in which they are drawn, their differences being the subject of the drawing. Style is a means of dating things culturally, and Steinberg juxtaposes styles of different times in order to create an awareness of the constant proliferation of anachronisms. A structure of machine forms in a post-Cubist still life, a plane containing Spencerian handwriting, a female figure composed of a bundle of dots call attention to different layers of cultural history that coexist in our time. Or he compresses his demonstration of anachronism into a Mondrian-like abstraction with a Douanier Rousseau signature.

In his shorthand of styles, Steinberg records the heritage of disparate moods to which current society is subject. His sober little man passes from an Impressionist sketch of a house in the sky down a ladder to a simple contour drawing of a house and over a bridge to a chain of concentric rings suspended in space (*Biography*, opposite, right). Discussing this drawing, Steinberg invites the spectator to collaborate with him by discovering in it any meaning that occurs to him — in sum, to explore within himself the feelings aroused by this encounter with the three prominent modes of aesthetic statement constituting the drawing. For his own part, Steinberg offers the explanation that "it means that evolution doesn't lead to perfection but to the invention or discovery of new regions." (To speak of the "invention" of a region is pure Steinberg.) With or without evolution, the three distinct styles in which the drawing is composed synchronize three cultural time periods and their characteristic emotional colorations: sexual, practical, mechanical.

Varieties of style-jamming appear in numerous Steinberg drawings, such as the assembly of a dozen chairs composed of penmanship decorations in designs from African woven to Eames chromium. A couple seated side by side on a sofa are separated forever by the fact that she consists of a shower of short pencil strokes, he of thick contours. Avant-garde artists seeking a style exclusively appropriate to the present day exclude masses of existing phenomena, from subjects too often seen in the art of the past (apples on a plate) to out-of-date furniture, scenes and people. One reason that Steinberg's drawings appeal to such a wide public is that in them the twentieth century is as rich in leftovers as a flea market or a boardinghouse parlor. The general atmosphere of his drawings is Victorian, even in his architectural fantasies of Las Vegas and science fiction. He likes plazas and Grand Hotels, busts and potted plants, admirals covered with medals, birds in cages, gold-leaf lettering, ladies' hats with fruit and plumage, monarchs and grandees of small countries (his America is a small country). These, plus men in armor, animals in armor (crocodiles) and fruit in armor (pineapples), are obliged to accommodate themselves to robots and rockets and Cities of the Future. Like Joyce, Steinberg appropriates styles wherever he finds them, whether on the midway or in the museum, and refits them through parody as expressions of contemporary experience. His ever-active little man is kin to Here Comes Everybody of *Finnegans Wake* and is subject to HCE's countless dreamy reidentifications.

Style, with its power of creating assent, is society's major instrument of deception—authoritarian governments are more violently outraged by rebellions against the officially approved manner in the arts than by the depiction of unwelcome subjects. Each mode in art is, in its beginnings, the realization of a mood or sentiment—for example, Rembrandt-like depth in contrast to Art Nouveau chic or Impressionist vivacity. This characteristic mood remains sealed into the images done in the given style, whether in its masterpieces, in its run-of-the-mill creations or, finally, in its mass-produced imitations. As the style keeps reappearing, however, in works of diminishing quality and in printed copies, its emotional content is coarsened and reduced to effects induced by its most easily recognized features, as in the piled-on paint of late Abstract Expressionist "10th Street" paintings. Thus the style survives in parodies or masquerades of the original feelings embedded in them.

Steinberg grasps the power secreted in styles regardless of their status as art. Degraded styles, including the junky ornamentation of city life as well as grand modes abandoned by sophisticated tastes, are welded to the masterworks of the past, on the one hand, and to the aesthetic reflexes of the public, on the other. Steinberg understands the history of art as a form language of ready-made sentiments, at once self-evident and spurious, situated on the border of comedy and nostalgia, like the beard of Santa Claus or the red heart of a valentine. Steinberg's analysis of pictorial conventions on every level, from Kasimir Malevich's to those of anonymous tattooers, is his recoupment of the past. Art history in its actual survival into present-day existence as the content of museum catalogues, varnish-darkened family portraits and Cubist masks is the ideal vocabulary for a pictorial autobiography in which to recall feelings without giving details. "My drawing," said Steinberg, "contains often parodies of drawing. It's a form of art criticism." He refers to a drawing (*Biography*) that "shows a man crossing from one technique to another, or from one meaning to another." And for him this transition represents "conflicts, emotions."

The decline of art into popular decorations and emotional stimulants is a major source of Steinberg's philosophical comedy, as it was for Duchamp in painting a mustache and goatee on a reproduction of Leonardo's *Mona Lisa*. Steinberg collects bad art, such as the tapestries sold in Broadway close-out shops, though the ones he chooses always have something special about them. He sees this kitsch as the legacy inherited by the modern world from the art of earlier centuries. Religious and romantic motifs—Madonnas, a lion attacking a mounted African warrior, a stag reflected in a lake—are made into low-priced designs. The French, he explains, have a word for this stuff: *bondieuserie*, which comes from *bon Dieu*. "All that region behind Saint-Sulpice in Paris is a big center for selling plaster-cast Jesuses, sweet Madonnas, and so on. So many things become *bondieuserie* in the end—respectable and beautiful, but comical because they

are such clichés." Each artist's work, whether he is aware of it or not, is subject to conversion into clichés—and he himself is subject to the same transformation. A frequently reproduced Steinberg shows an artist at his easel inside the jaws of a crocodile. "The crocodile is Aztec. It has the rigidity of extinction." This animal is Steinberg's symbol of an insatiable society that gobbles up everything, including works of art that are digested into a common breakfast food of the emotions. It is society that makes forms stiff, lifeless and repetitive. In time, the distance between the researches into self of Pollock, de Kooning, Newman and Steinberg's autobiographical explication of visual clichés was bound to narrow, as the works of the former overcame their estrangement from the public consciousness and achieved the familiarity of a comic strip. In Steinberg's universe, the alternative is either to begin with a cliché or to end as one. Like Baudelaire, he sees the cliché as formed by endless human movements within the same rut, thus adumbrating depths of meaning.

Steinberg's early drawings tend to gain their effects through visual jokes and surprises. An artist painting an EXIT sign with a pointing finger uses his own pointing finger as a model. A man holds up a child to look at the moon as if it were a parade (*The Moon*, page 28). In an art gallery, a crush of spectators fights to get a peek at the painting of a solitary figure in a desert (a motif, incidentally, of Steinberg's late watercolors and canvases). A nude is painted on a bathtub as

if half immersed in painted water but with her head out of it. Another woman is painted on the back of a chair and on the seat. Musical staff paper held horizontally supplies an elastic exerciser for a man drawn on it; held vertically, its lines rain down on a pedestrian. Music paper also provides the ground for Expressionist drawings in heavy lines of musicians and dancing couples. Fairly early, too, are drawings of signatures changed into things that are carried around like constructions made of steel bands and wires.

Inventions extending into Steinberg's middle period are his signs (e.g., the question mark) and speech and sound structures that acquire the substantiality of objects and creatures. Thus visual effects of drawing, popular art, handwriting acquire new life through new uses. A horizontal line keeps changing its functions—from a table edge it turns into a railroad trestle, then into a laundry line with clothes hung on it, finally an abstract flourish (*The Line*). The devices of drawing place the real, the imaginary and the abstract on the same plane of being. A question mark arises as a sign above the little man's head. It becomes an object that, on another occasion, he carries under his arm like a piece of furniture. Again, he holds an armful of question marks like a bouquet of flowers.

One of Steinberg's richest veins has been his elaboration of the comic-strip balloon. With Steinberg, the usual oval outline in which speech is rendered visually has been transformed into varieties of shapes and substances that are both things in themselves and also suggest the quality of the statements, their sounds, their aesthetic and emotional effects. The balloons take on materiality—they are held in the hand like platters or tennis rackets. They turn into animals that swallow the speeches of others. They are joined by the speech of cannons, which is blasted apart by the rocket of a mathematical formula. A speaker himself turns into a balloon loaded with sheets of script that dart out of his mouth as though he were a coin machine. Out of the mouths of ephemeral persons come huge constructions of words, complex clockworks of reflections, solid grills, architectural ornaments; a dog barks a fierce zigzag; a piano builds a cascade of hatchings; a cellist leaks a spreading worm of black; on a mountain of gibberish that he is in the process of enunciating gesticulates an orator who is a scribble. Sitting behind his desk, an authoritative gentleman directs at a petitioner a screen of discourse that takes the shape of NO. A tuba releases a baroque plaster ornament of sound, a horn ejaculates an aural flowerpot, a cymbal scatters stars and seed formations. In a family discussion (*Three Speeches*), the daughter's plantlike statement competes with her father's severe geometrical edifice and her mother's mollifying string of jewels and feathers (page 28).

Having risen to the status of three-dimensional entities, the speech balloons take to meeting secretly in hotel bedrooms (*Hotel Plaka*, page 13). Perhaps as a result, the balloons develop images within themselves that in turn produce their own speech balloons, indicating that talk and its imagery result in thoughts that have thoughts of their own—layers of consciousness that again suggest Joyce. Steinberg has expanded the cartoon balloon into a means for dramatic monologue: a thin scratchy female emits a balloon containing the bust of a woman from whose mouth emerges a

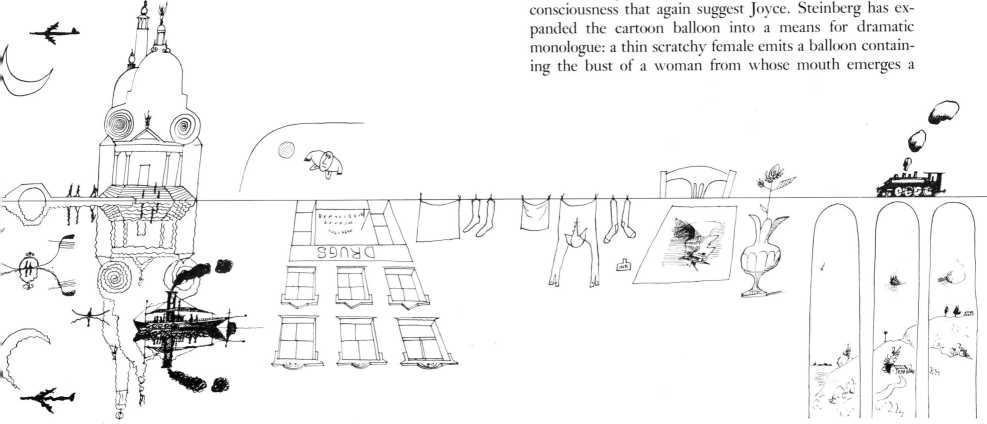

balloon of inverted script and above whose head ascend bubbles (indicating thought) leading to a balloon in which a man in a landscape speaks a balloon-enclosed message. The spectator can reach his own conclusion as to what the woman protagonist is saying and what the woman she is talking about is thinking. Interpreted "politically," the speech structures can often be seen as forming barriers between speakers and their hearers, rather than communications. At times a speech replaces the forepart of a speaker's head, leaving only a design.

Counterpointing the materialization of speech and sound, words behave as "characters" who undergo experiences derived from their own meaning, as in the incomparable series of drawings in which SICK lies flattened out on a couch, HELP! topples off a cliff, TANTRUM explodes into a rocket display. Steinberg's personified words reflect, decide, march in formation, choose directions. On the rocky formation of I AM is balanced a flimsy wooden I HAVE, while in the sky above whizzes a dynamic I DO.

Steinberg's personifications provide a means of approach to the thinking from which his images are formed. In his later works, his drawings have become increasingly philosophical and abstract and this has brought them into closer relation with words, as in the examples of word-actions mentioned above. The jokes still leap out of the images, but they hint at more complex interpretations than the drawings of nudes on the verge of slipping into bathtubs. The late drawings tend to present themselves as visual incidents in a complex mental happening; they are the outcome of the kind of unique reasoning that one encounters in Steinberg's talk. Beginning with an abstract proposition, his discourse heats up through associations of ideas until its chemical mixture gives rise to the fading in of an image as in a decalcomania. The pen of the artist-monologist brings into being pictures that strain toward a concept but are incapable of reaching it, like the dog-artist in a Steinberg who is trying to leap at his easel but is kept at a distance from it by a rope around his neck.

Steinberg sets the spectator's mind to work and keeps it going by frustrating his desire to reach a conclusion. A word, a number can now be analyzed as a hypothetical situation seen in dramatic perspective. A cat with his head poked into the upper part of a wire number 4 planted in the ground is the product of the following Steinbergian analysis of the digits as material shapes—an analysis carried on from the point of view of cats as creatures famous for (that is, labeled with the cliché of) their curiosity (*Cat and 4*). "Four is an interesting number because it is a shape that would arouse the curiosity of a cat. Most numbers are either open or closed. Number 8, for instance, is closed; a cat has no

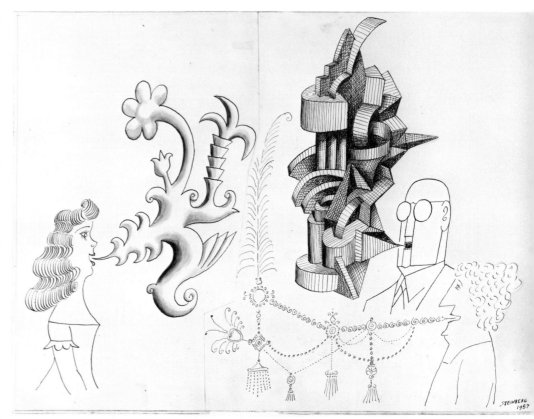

New Yorker Passport ST 19

New Yorker New World   ST 1962

business to look inside. A cat likes to peer into something that is half open—a little bit open—a mystery. Number 3 is obvious; number 1 is nothing; 5 perhaps is more intriguing, but 4 certainly is perfectly designed and engineered for a cat to look inside and find out what is going on. So here I combined an illusion of reality with an abstraction. The abstraction, number 4, became a reality and the cat became an abstraction because it combined itself with this number. It rendered the whole thing plausible and, from a drawing point of view, perfectly workable."

Readers of this vaudeville monologue in the high style of comic rationality may become aware that the number 4 is being dealt with as a shape that has been deprived of its function in the numerical system and has "become a reality." It is a found object of the same order as a tree or a tin can. This metaphysical reordering of the familiar is a resource of Steinberg's imagination that places him in the forefront of later artists, such as Jasper Johns, who have also conceived ready-made signs as material objects. In staging the cat as a seeker of the digit best suited to its objectively conceived personality, Steinberg adds a psychological dimension to his drawing that is lacking in the aestheticism of Johns's number paintings with their references confined to art history—that is, to Abstract Expressionist paint handling and *I Saw the Figure 5 in Gold*, by Charles Demuth.

Another drawing of the same period draws on a theme that appears throughout Steinberg's work, the theme of fame and its constriction of life. The drawing is an abstract biography developed out of the parentheses in which vital statistics are supplied on tombstones and in encyclopedias. *Between Parentheses* is a landscape with flowers in the foreground, above which rises a parenthesis in which 1905 is followed by a hyphen. After the hyphen, instead of a second date comes Steinberg's little man, who is about to be crowned by a bird with a laurel wreath. Steinberg explains that "this is the portrait of a famous man. He was born in 1905—and he is still alive. He walks, followed by his birthday and facing his

death day. That dash [the hyphen] hints at his end, eagerly awaited by historians who can thus officially close the parentheses. The essential thing about him, and this is the essence of his fame, is that he is between parentheses. He is not free. This monumentalization of people, this freezing of life, is the terrible curse of consciousness of fame. Anybody with instinct destroys conventional fame and misleads his admirers and biographers by being unreliable and therefore unpleasant. This gives him the possibility of looking instead of being looked at." Obviously, this explanation of the drawing is a passage of autobiography, although the drawing lives up to Steinberg's principle of disguise by "misleading" spectators with the wrong birthday.

A final example of Steinberg's rare public analyses of his drawings presents the free-ranging associations out of which his drawings spring into being. "A giant rabbit is being attacked by a hero on a horse. But the mark of the hero is the size and quality he picks out for himself to fight. Any hero who fights a rabbit is not so good. What is a giant rabbit? It is weakness carried to an enormous degree. Maybe it has to be destroyed. I made another drawing of a hero fighting a giant baby. A giant baby can be very dangerous. You cannot reason with him: he cannot be controlled. If we were subjected to 6-month-old babies with iron muscles, we would all be murdered. There is something equally dangerous about the giant rabbit, but should he be destroyed, or should he be educated? Anyway, it is a moral situation. But many people thought it had to do with sex and I'm not surprised" (page 30). The drawing plus the interpretation constitutes a metaphysical fable, one relating to the Nietzschean issue of the menace of the feeble. Steinberg's picture-plus-words illustrates how he derives ideas from manipulating the meaning-laden figures he has developed over the years—knights, rabbits, cats, little men—at the same time that he augments the significance, private and public, of these originally commonplace images.

Drawing is a way of reasoning on paper.
— SAUL STEINBERG

Steinberg has insisted that his own interpretations of his drawings are not the only ones possible. As noted, he regards the spectator as his collaborator. Yet the view persists that Steinberg's drawings express a systematic outlook toward life today. Especially among Europeans, he is an irresistible source for composers of existentialist sermons. His drawings are held to depict the absurdity and isolation of modern man and to point to an all-encompassing pessimism. Do not his ever-active abstractions—a wiry YES assaulting an imperturbable NO; his representations of man (*Comic Strip*, 1958, page 47) as disintegrating into every conceivable slapstick absurdity of thought, speech, motion, feeling, including, in one frame of animal figures, a hint of Picasso's *Dream and Lie of Franco*—state propositions that add up to a black view of the human condition? Steinberg has confessed to a Mozartian "seriousness, or melancholy, camouflaged as gaiety," and it is true that some of his social panoramas of the past few years—such as *Law and Order* and *Street War* (pages 152 and 126)—have a grim tone. In a one-line cartoon, the artist draws himself into a circle. Since the line starts with the head, the drawing may be interpreted to mean that to begin with reason is to tie oneself up in a never-ending line, a labyrinth of arguments, which the thinker-artist renders more complex and difficult to escape from with each move he makes. The drawing could be taken to represent the history of civilized man. And so on.

Yet it is a mistake to believe that one can get to the bottom of Steinberg, that even Steinberg can. His drawings are to be understood not as illustrations of a doctrine or world view but as experiences in what he has described as the complicity of the contemporaneous. The drawing means to each spectator whatever he can find in it. Steinberg's art is an act that brings forth an insight, at times in the form of a riddle, and in return demands an act of comprehension. Too much interpretation makes this responsive act more difficult. "Every explanation," said Steinberg, "is over-explanation." Despite the popular imagery on which his art is based, it is, in the end, as gnomic as that of his Abstract Expressionist contemporaries.

Steinberg copes with his present experience by circling back to earlier phases of his art and re-creating their language for new purposes. His Tables of the 1970s are assemblages on boards of pictures and handmade, eye-fooling fakes of his art instruments—pens, pencils, brushes, rulers, drawing pads, notebooks—plus such trademarks as his speech balloons and rubber-stamp seals, which serve the same function of identification as his fingerprints and official signatures of the 1950s. The largest of the boards are mounted on sawhorses and become actual tables. As neatly arranged as in the showcases of a police agency, the implements of Steinberg's art represent another plane of his autobiography, the objects of his deepest emotional attachment—his "erotica," as he likes to call them. These objects have been rendered more intimate than the usual studio materials of an artist by the fact that they are not merely things the artist has used but simulacra of them which he has made. They are extensions of himself yet, like his paper-bag masks, "not reality but a symbol." Once again, Steinberg presents a fabrication that stands for him but also hides him. The Tables continue his autobiography in personal terms that betray no secrets.

Steinberg began the Tables by idly whittling wooden copies of pencils, paintbrushes and drawing pads and painting them to resemble the real things. Unlike Cubist, Dada and Surrealist collage, nothing in the Tables is a found object, though most of their original content—that is, the stuff copied—could have been obtained in an art-supply store. The paraphernalia of the studio connect the artist and his creations, hence are objects that symbolize their subject. Their subjectivity is underscored in the Tables by the fact that they were not taken from the real world but were created by the artist. In putting together these whittlings as objects to be exhibited, Steinberg assembled bits of himself—his organs, so to speak. The Tables offer to the public reproductions of things grown intimate to the artist through daily use. Those enclosed in Plexiglas are a parody of objects in the display cases of a museum. The satire includes the bitter point that in making himself visible the artist is also entombed by the same means—a point related to Steinberg's drawing of the famous man in the parentheses.

Arranged in symmetrical groupings, as if by a neat head clerk, the contents of the Tables have an atmosphere of administrative order. But not of today's administrator—they convey the nostalgia of offices supplied with worn wooden penholders, chewed pencil stubs, imported bonbon boxes used to hold paper clips.

As collections of memorabilia, Steinberg's Tables are comparable to Duchamp's *Valise*, which enabled the artist to carry his past with him to the United States in the form of reproductions of his paintings and a phial of air of Paris, an equivalent to the grandmother's featherbed brought by other immigrants. In regard to nostalgia, Steinberg's Tables are much less emotionally incriminating than *Valise*, since they cope with the artist's attachment to his past not through preserving representations of things done and objects valued but through counterfeits of them by which they are both memorialized and falsified. The faked nostalgia of Steinberg's Tables is less nostalgic than the real nostalgia of Duchamp's *Valise*, hence less sentimental and more "modern." Steinberg's nostalgia is there but is ameliorated through new acts of creation. The Table called *Portrait* recapitulates his odyssey in typical Steinberg shorthand. In

the upper right-hand corner, a plaque labeled "Milan, 1935" commemorates the city where Steinberg began his career as an artist and the date when he arrived there. A wooden cutout of a comic-strip balloon inscribed with a seal and illegible handwriting represents floating speech without a speaker, perhaps the talking Steinberg engaged in during those voluble student years. A fake pen, pencils, brushes and a ledger are relics of the artist at work. An open page of a faked drawing pad shows a pencil portrait of the young woman who is the artist's present companion. Symbols of Steinberg's active life, they have the advantage that they will never be used up as are the actual implements of the artist but, like his paper-bag mask in contrast to a snapshot, are "something steady that I made."

Steinberg is a craftsman whose skill drifts into ideas and through them into visual enigmas. Yet he frequently makes drawings and paintings for the sheer pleasure of putting the hand in the service of the eye. *Country Still Life* is a lyrical drawing in colored pencil of flowers in a vase, a bottle and a pitcher set against a view through the glass doors of Steinberg's living room in East Hampton. A more recent drawing, *Still Life Cover*, though it includes elements of the

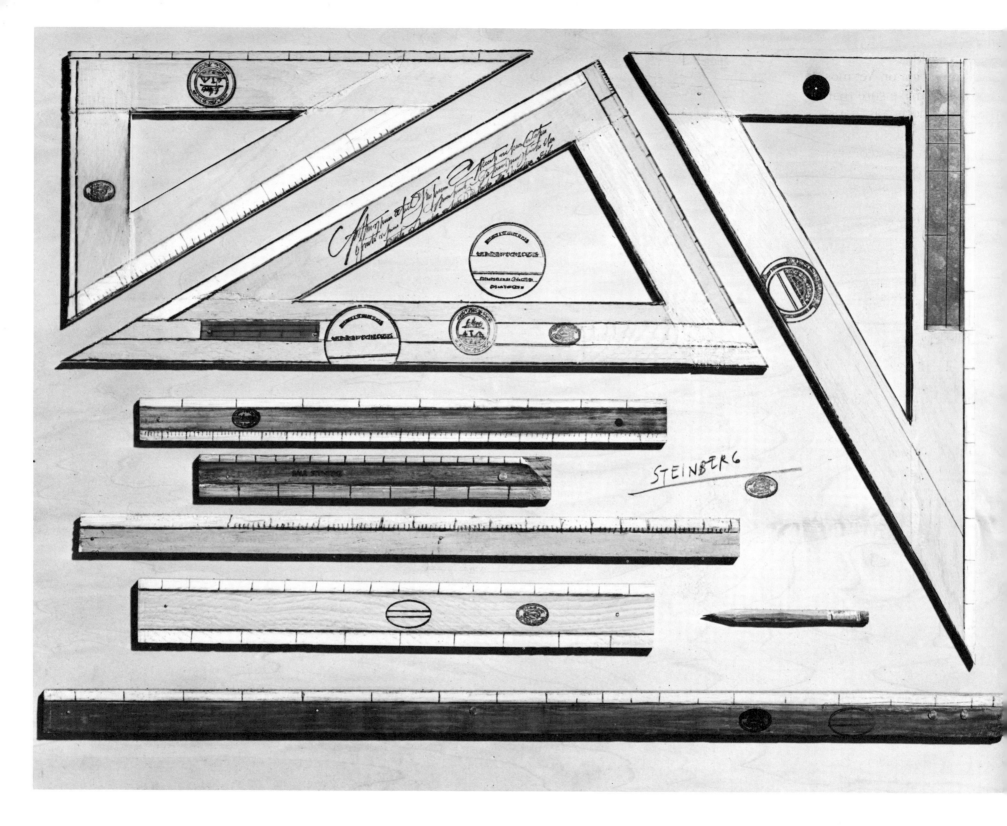

Tables, similarly makes no intellectual demands on the spectator. Yet most spectators will scrutinize them with care to make sure that these pictures, given their author, are as innocent as they seem.

Related to these pictures, which—compared to the often recondite conceptions of his cartoons and collages—were produced for nonintellectual pleasure, are Steinberg's landscape souvenirs of recent travels, which he calls "postcards." They differ from Steinberg's earlier travel drawings in that they make no overt effort to seize the essence of a particular place. The watercolors and oil-on-paper landscapes of the 1970s convey overtones of nostalgia through touches of stylistic anachronism and visions of loneliness.

By externalizing and depersonalizing his feelings, Steinberg causes estrangement itself to be estranged and made to belong to other times, thus avoiding romantic self-expression. Many of the "postcard" landscapes bear rubber-stamped insignia floating in the sky like gasbags or planets; these may be intended as evidence that the landscapes are "documents," stamped on their way through Steinberg's metaphysical post office and certified as authentic by the authorities that rule his made-up world.

Another oddity of some of the landscapes is their division horizontally into one or more separate scenes, as if they were photographs taken at different times—a typical Steinberg adaptation of another medium. In their drab enunciation of details, they might be illustrations accompanying an old report of a surveying expedition or an oil-drilling operation. In some of the landscapes there are queer-looking machines with buildings in the background, and in front of them barely perceptible figures whose costumes suggest that they are either natives or adventuring Westerners. They confront the spectator full face, as if getting their pictures taken, or stand with their backs to him waiting in what might be a desert. Where these activities occurred and what happened, if anything, cannot be determined from the paintings, but a sense of distant places is conveyed by such titles as *Abu Dabu, Kunming* and *Ottumwa*, which sound Asian or African, though Ottumwa is actually in Iowa.

Some of the landscapes identify themselves as Egyptian by pyramids towering in the background, while another kind depicts scenes on Long Island in the luminist style common in nineteenth-century American landscape painting. In one group of paintings, low-lying foregrounds and immense empty skies with a pinkish-yellow glow at the horizon mimic the shoreline panoramas of America's age of exploration and pioneering, an age to which, it may be presumed, Steinberg feels he still belongs. His rubber-stamped (in oil paint, not

ink) male figures placed along water edges or ground rises heighten the sense of loneliness; once more the immigrant artist has found a nostalgic self-reflection in the history of painting.

That Steinberg's art-making and philosophizing usually "masquerade as cartoons" (as he puts it) suggests that he is to an unusual degree conscious of his audience, both the worldwide general public, whom most artists tend to ignore, and the gallery-going public, which is the social core of the art world. Steinberg finds in the latter types comparable to Hollywood cowboys, high steppers and stylized females at bingo games. Spectators in art galleries and the paintings that confront them on the walls bear the social "imprint" of common styles, thus meet as mirror reflections of one another. In *Art Lovers* (1965), the figures of the female spectators merge with the forms within the frames through projecting the eyeball and cranium of the woman on the right onto the picture plane and extending the bottom edge of the frame in the left section to include the other spectator, and fitting her speech balloon to the right edge of the frame. Another aspect of Steinberg's gallery drawings are his mimic exhibitions presented in an illusion of perspective by means of vertical pictures that grow narrower and shorter toward the center in order to form an imaginary corridor of painting (*The Collection*, page 35).

Steinberg's merger of the spectator with the work of art is an instance of the tendency in our time for real things to cross over into fiction—and of fictions to be transformed into realities. People and events become indistinguishable from fabricated versions of them that are distributed by the mass media. The history of the last war exists in the public mind as the sum total of popular war movies, while the next war is already under way as depicted in best-seller spy narratives. We have entered an epoch in which nothing is real until it is reproduced. This mixing of fact and fiction is one of the most powerful determinants of form in modern art, as it is, too, of behavior in politics and diplomacy. Art has found ways to transfer raw data into painting and sculpture by adulterating the first with paste-ins (collage), the second with the incorporation of ready-made objects. Yet while functioning on the edge where art blends into existence, artists have been unable to purge themselves of the ambition for masterpieces that dwell on the plane of the timeless. Repudiating a metaphysically separated realm of Beauty, they nevertheless strive to insure the future destiny of their creations as treasures of the museum. This conflict of motives often turns art into a confidence game, in which clumsy works are defended in the name of truth and empty ones in the name of art history.

Steinberg's borderline experience—geographical, psychological, aesthetic—has made him an adept of the postwar consciousness. From the start, he has gone the whole way in dissociating himself from the pieties of art. Among the first to recognize that the contemporary art museum and the popular magazine are engaged in related projects of mass culture, he cut around the morass of the artist as culture hero by going over completely into art intended for reproduction. In the lowly cartoon he found a medium susceptible of being transformed into an alphabet of meanings as flexible as that of words but with the additional dimension of the visual sign. Borderline experiences demand borderline forms. The intellectual potential of drawings made for publication lay precisely in their being a *modest* medium, in which the spectator responds to the artist's statement without requiring that it satisfy ideals of aesthetic prestige.

While retaining the cartoon as the nucleus of his art, Steinberg has vastly enlarged its scope with ideas, techniques, approaches derived from the history of art and from twentieth-century art in particular: automatic drawing ("the doodle is the brooding of the hand"), drawings by children and the mentally disturbed, naïve art, scrawls on walls and latrines, facsimiles, transferred images (drawings on photographs), parodies of modern and old masters. In works to be printed he resuscitated handwriting, thus turning progress inside out. The Steinbergian metamorphosis of the cartoon into a vehicle for meditating on a seemingly limitless range of issues, including the central ones of art—illusion, self and reality—constitutes an expansion of the intellectual resources of flat-surface composition comparable to that of collage. In his hands the cartoon is made to serve as a major medium. Through forms of representation until recently alien to the museum tradition but present in art since the beginnings of graphic expression, he has forged a means by which to animate areas of the mind outside those chloroformed by the tradition of Great Works.

As noted, Steinberg has been growing increasingly philosophical with the passage of the years. What is remarkable is how he has been able to expand his sign language to match the enlargement of his thought. He has developed an idiom that belongs among those rare recastings of available aesthetic "junk"—e.g., Picasso's assemblages—to serve the exact uses of a unique mind, that have brought new life to art in our time.

Steinberg straddles the contradictory functions that constitute the reality of art in our time: on the one hand, the use of art by the artist to lay bare the pattern of his individual identity; on the other, the making of objects for the art market and to win a place in art history (the museum). In Steinberg's autobiographical art, with its deliberate mis-

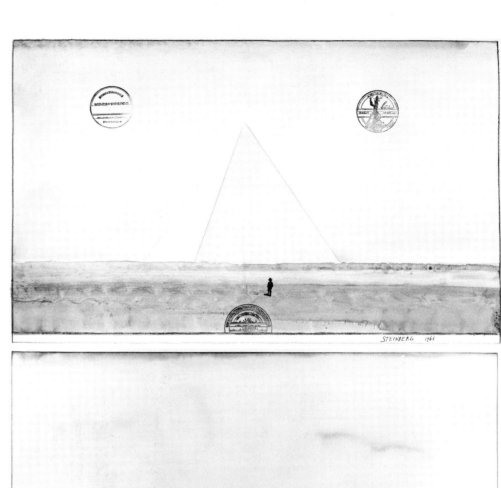

directions and false clues, these conflicting motives have been synthesized, symbolically and practically. Out of Steinberg's ironic saga of modern man as an abstract personage emerges the portrait of a unique individual, while his drawings have endeared themselves to admirers and collectors throughout the world by their elegance of execution—their "politeness," as Steinberg describes it.

Encompassing the dramatic polarities in the motives of creation today, Steinberg's art—with its copying, parodying, counterfeiting and mimicking—is also a central exhibit in the debate concerning the interchange between the art object and non-art fact (nature). In linking art to the modern consciousness no artist is more relevant than Steinberg. That he remains an art-world outsider is a problem that critical thinking in art must compel itself to confront. There may be significance, for example, in the fact that Steinberg is the only major artist in the United States who is not associated with any art movement or style, past or present. Nor has art history to date assigned a place to Steinberg, perhaps for the reason that he has swallowed its subject matter—the successive displacement of one style by another —and regurgitated it as a single mass of expressive leftovers existing in the present. Cubism, for example, which in the canon of the American art historian is the nucleus of twentieth-century formal development in painting, sculpture and drawing, is to Steinberg merely another detail in the pattern of modern mannerisms; in a landscape, he finds no difficulty in combining Cubist and Constructivist elements with an imitation van Gogh "self-portrait" wearing opaque green spectacles and a Steinberg seal on the subject's slouch hat.

Dissolving art history into its original imaginative components, Steinberg's drawings and paintings are, as he has said, "a form of art criticism" that places him at the outermost edge of current art consciousness, a Duchamp who has transcended anti-art by exposing the power of form-making on every level of human experience, from women's makeup to the unplanned, collective evolution of the letters of the alphabet. In theory, Steinberg is today's avant-garde, except that, by definition, a single individual cannot be a vanguard. Thus his role automatically disguises itself (in harmony with his other disguises), and his performances continue to prompt some to respond with "Yes, but is he really an artist?"—the question that has greeted each authentic avant-garde for the past hundred years. Other avant-gardists—Pollock, Newman, Warhol, scatter sculptors, conceptualists—succeeded in evoking this question for varying intervals, then were "naturalized" into art by the embrace of the museum. The genius of Steinberg is to have kept the question alive about himself for thirty-five years, and to have made it impossible for art to acknowledge his legitimacy without changing its conception of itself.

Plates

Bingo in Venice, California

STEINBERG
1953

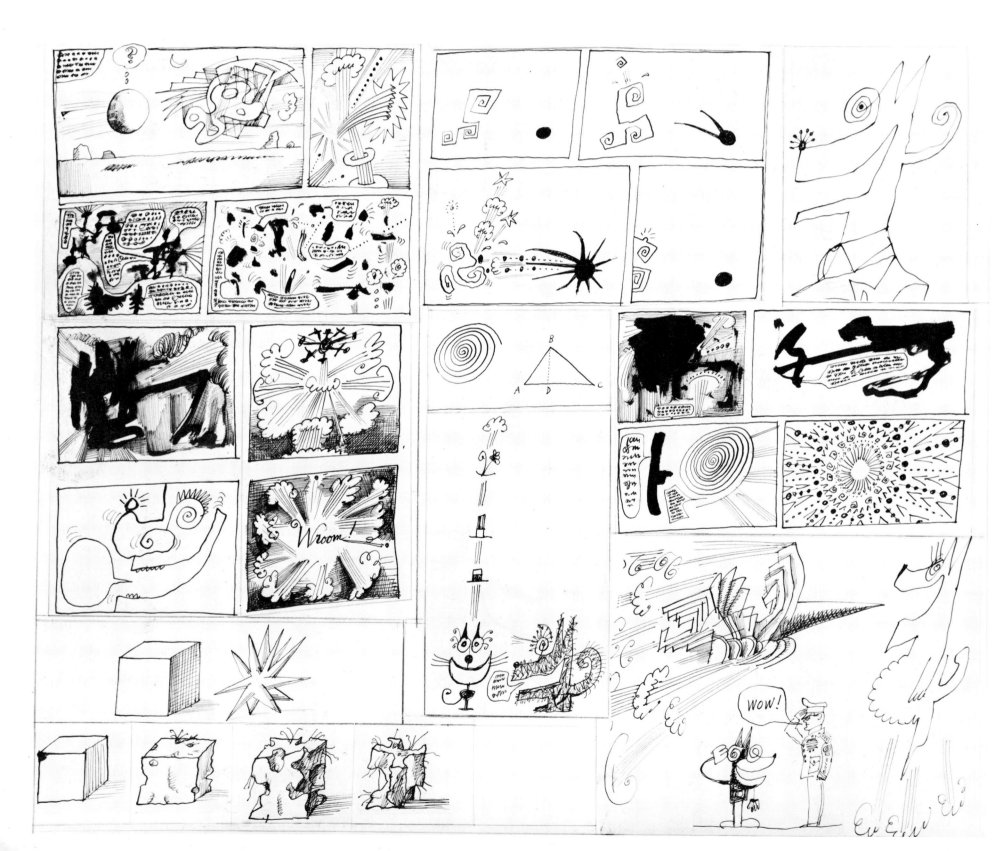

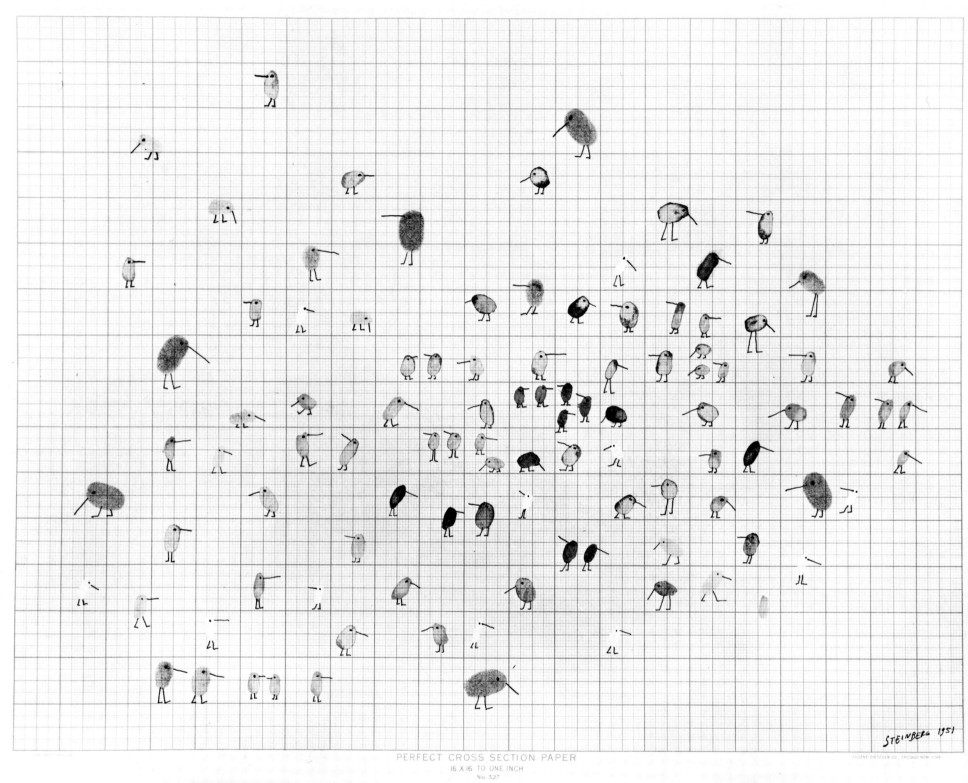

BIRDS ON GRAPH PAPER, 1951.

GRAPH PAPER BUILDING, 1950.
(Facing Page)

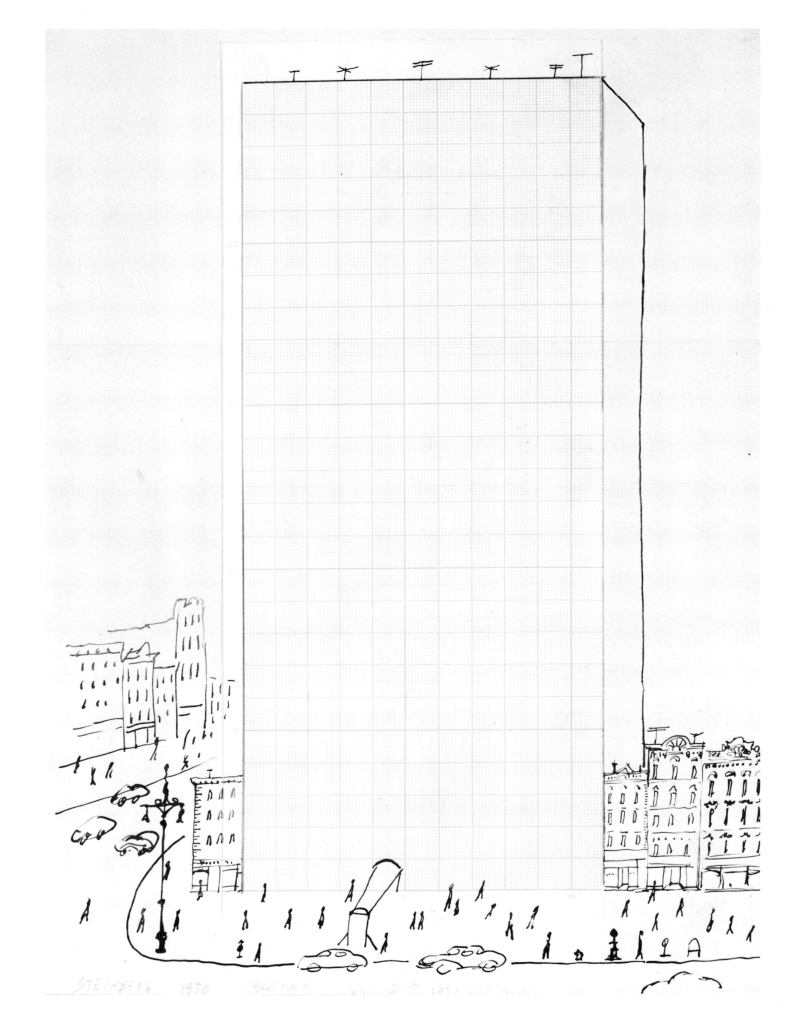

STEINBERG 1950

ST. 1951

53

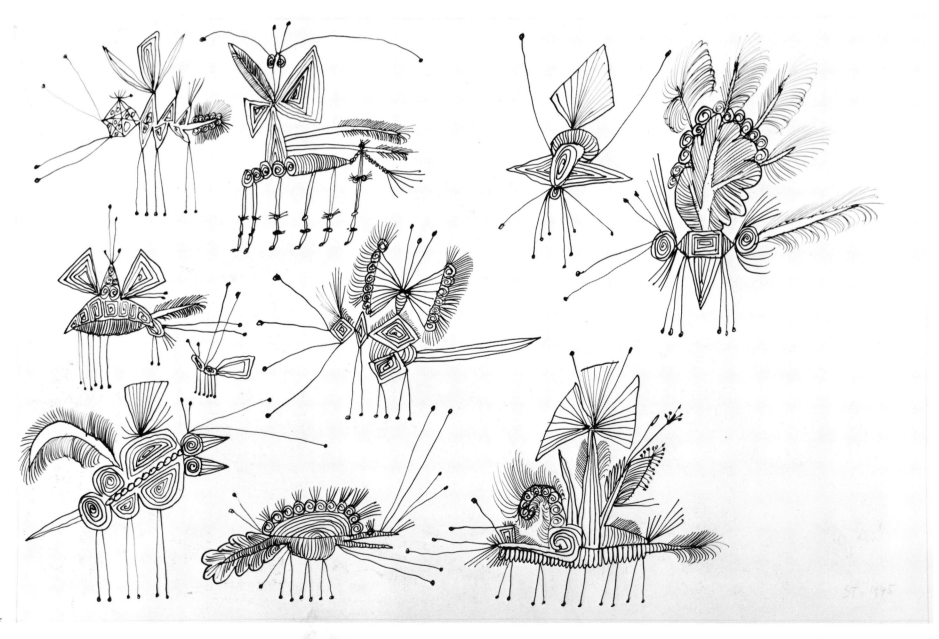

STEINBERG
1967

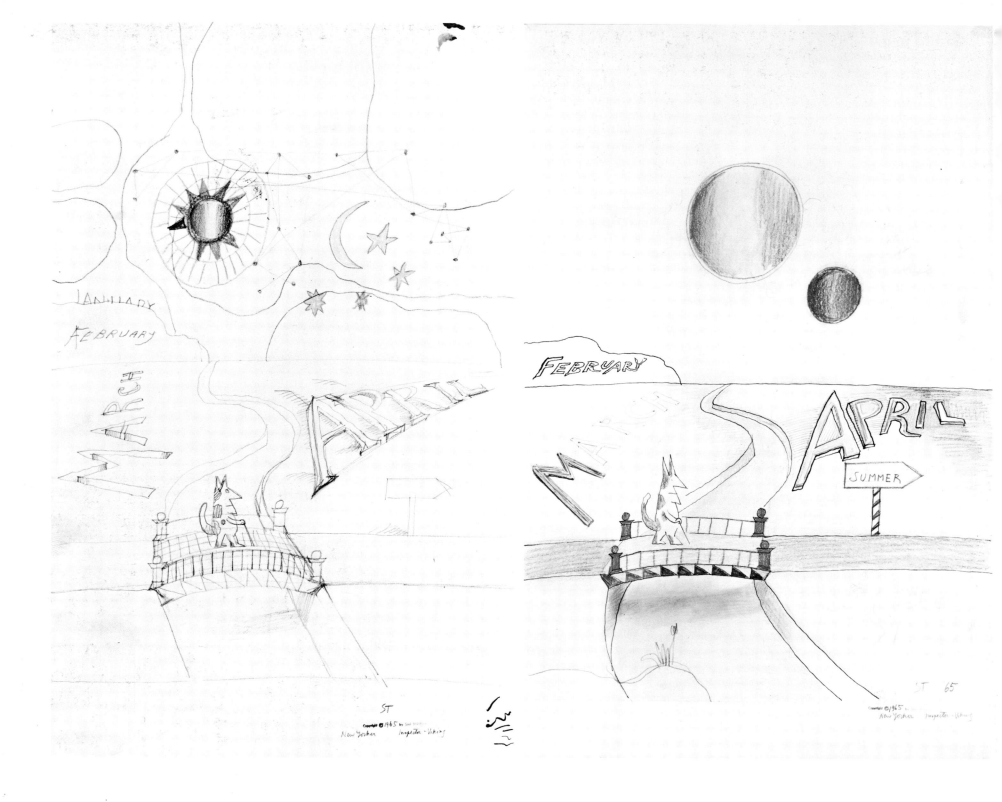

MARCH — APRIL VI, 1965.

MARCH — APRIL I, 1965.

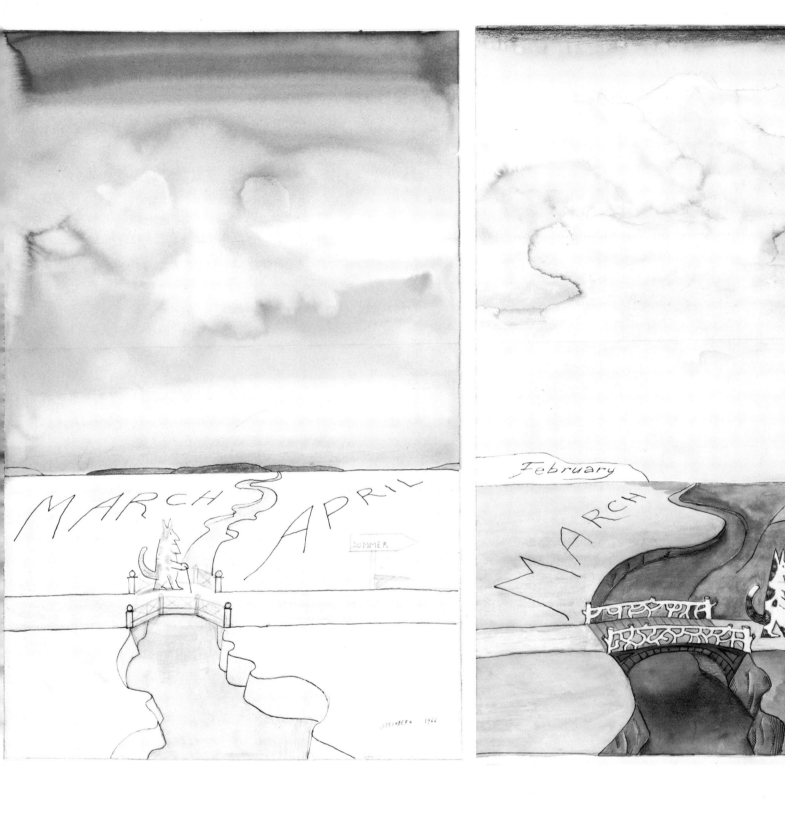

MARCH – APRIL IV, 1966.

MARCH – APRIL V, 1965.

SAM'S TROUBLES, 1960.
RIMBAUD DOCUMENT, 1953 (*detail*).

(Overleaf)

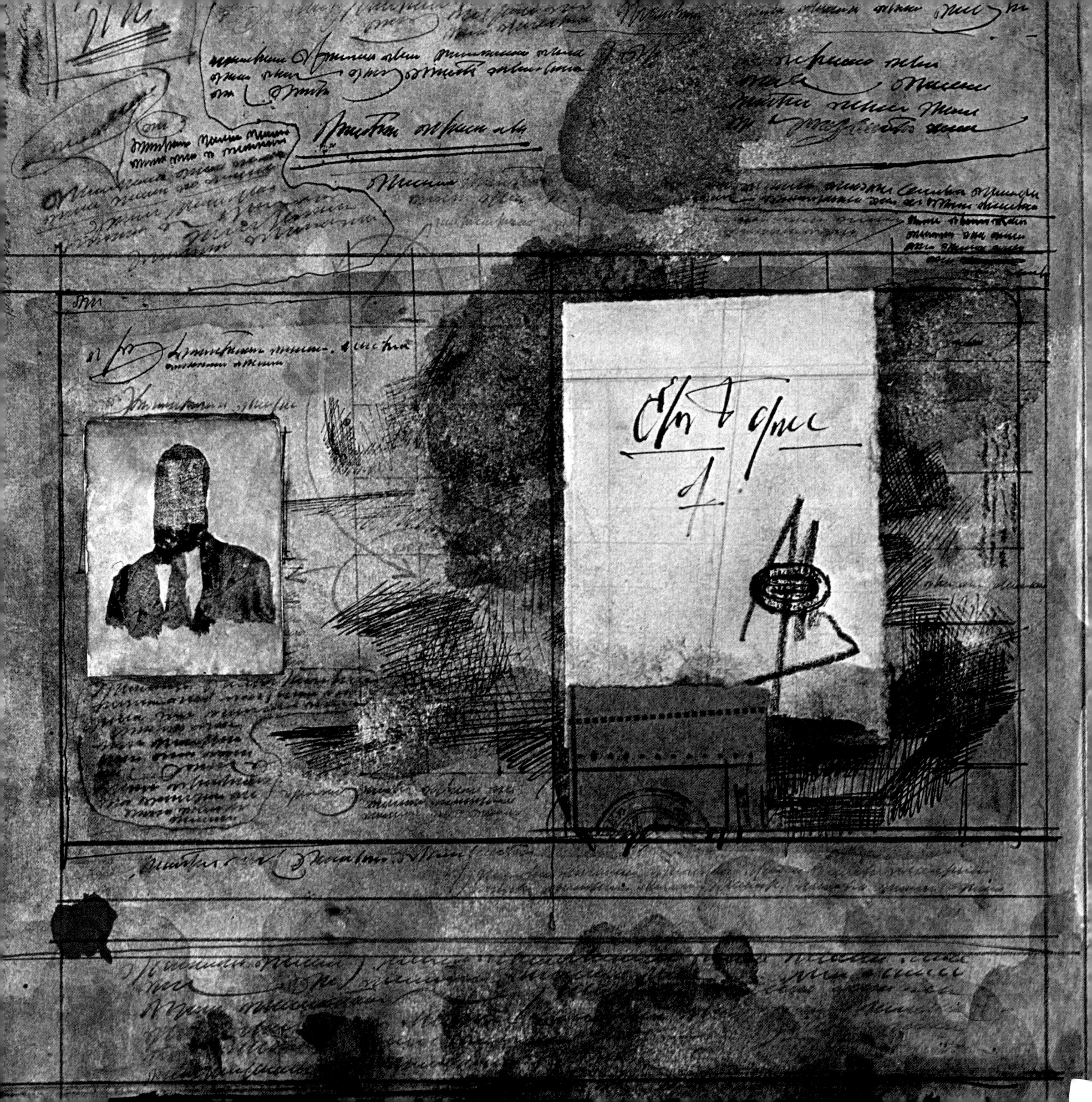

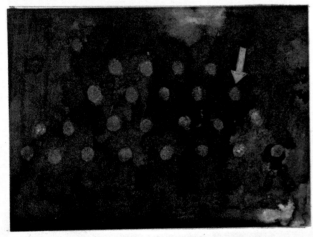

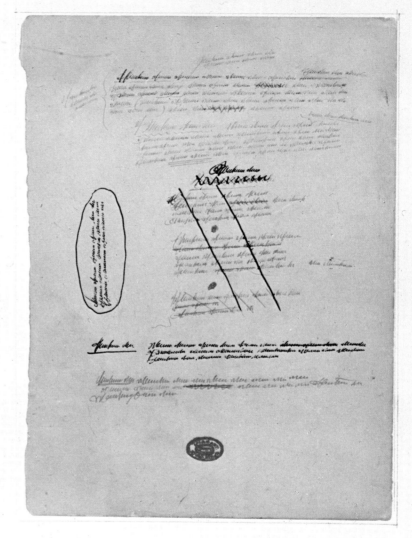

ALBUM, 1953 AND 1968.

EMIGRATION, 1965.

(Facing Page)

FABBRICA DI PASTORI, 1968.

INVENTORY, 1967.

PROSPERITY, 1959.
SHIP OF STATE (COVER B), 1959.
(Overleaf)

ENGINE, c. 1950.

FRENCH ENGINE, 1949.

NICE RAILWAY STATION, 1950.

GALLERIA DI MILANO, 1951.
VIEW OF THE WORLD FROM 9TH AVENUE, 1975.
(Overleaf)

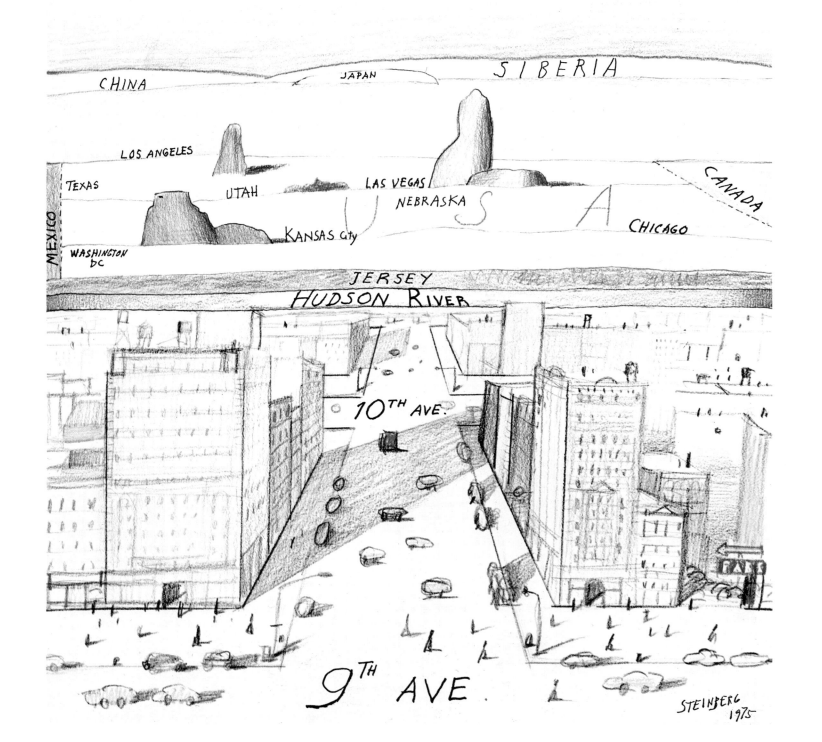

DINER

STEINBERG

(Facing Page)
JUKEBOX. 1965 *(detail)*.
DINER GIRL, 1971.

STEINBERG 1967

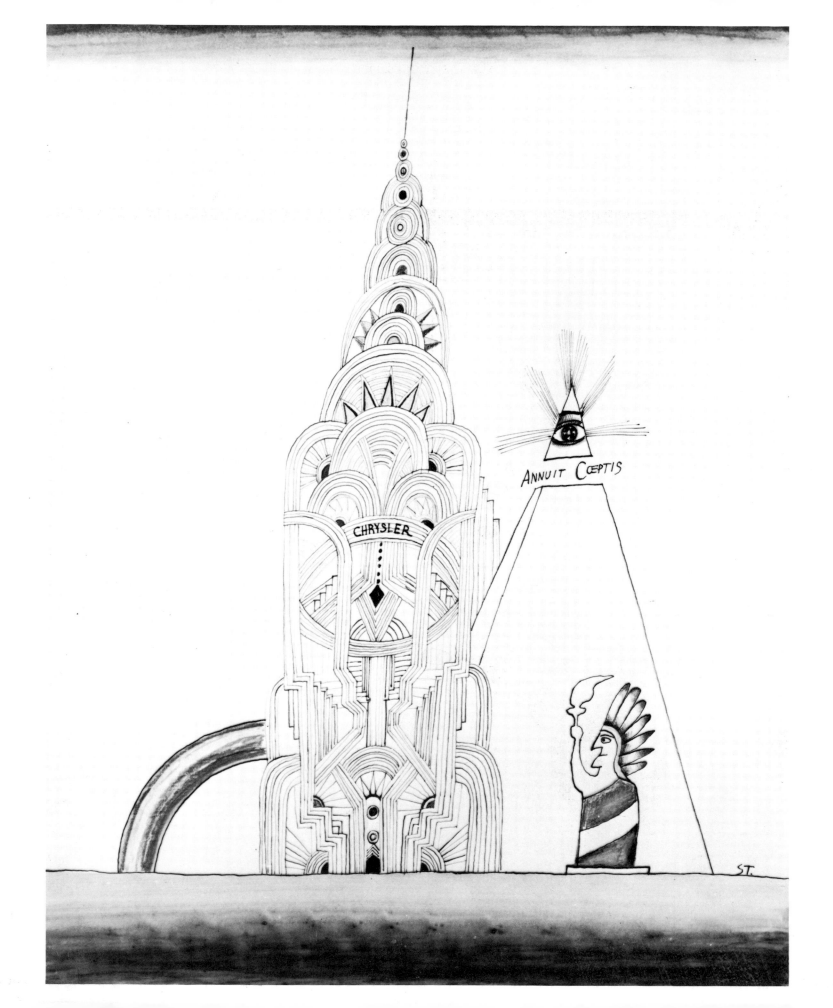

DEALERS, 1966.

GALLERY, 1966.

BAUHAUS DIALOGUE, 1969.

SAMURAI, 1966.
BLEECKER STREET, 1971 *(detail)*.
(Overleaf)

STEINBERG
1966

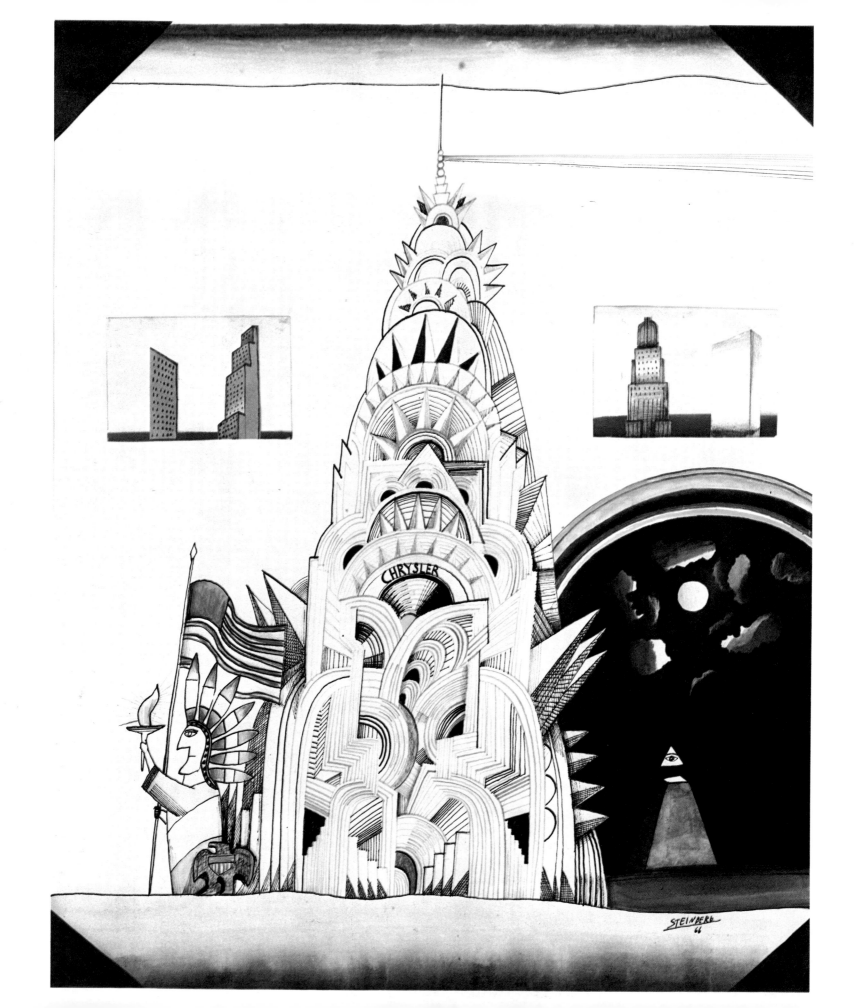

(Facing Page)
NEW YORK SKYLINE, 1966.
NEW YORK COPS, 1964.
BLEECKER STREET, 1969.
GAMBLERS I AND II, 1951.
(Overleaf)

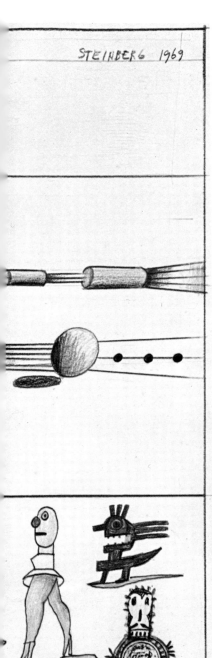

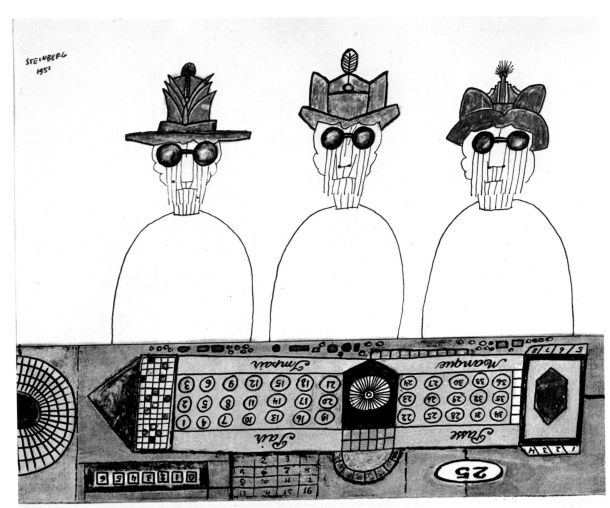

KOSMOS

STEINBERG
1969

BANK STREET, 1975.

DANCING COUPLE, 1965.
SIX TERRORISTS, 1971.
BONBON FABRIKA, 1972.
(Preceding Pages)

STEINBERG 1974

CAIRO, 1974.

EIGHTH STREET, 1966.

THE TREE, 1970.

STEINBERG 1952

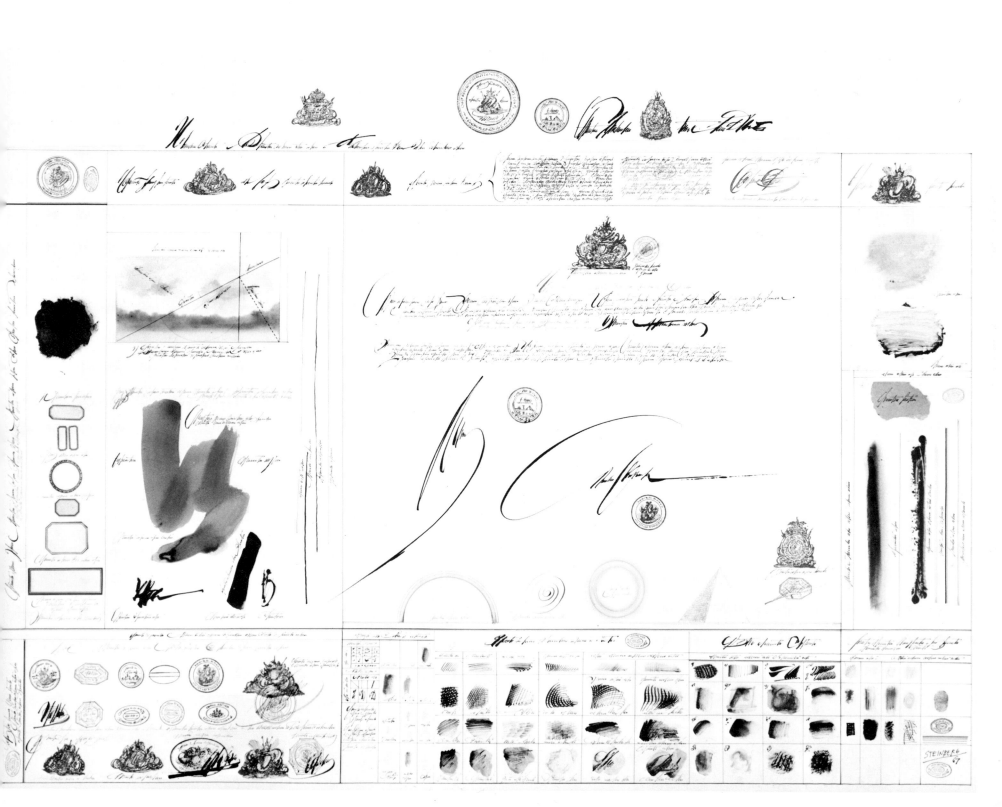

JOINT DECLARATION, 1966.

DOCUMENT, 1952.
(Facing Page)

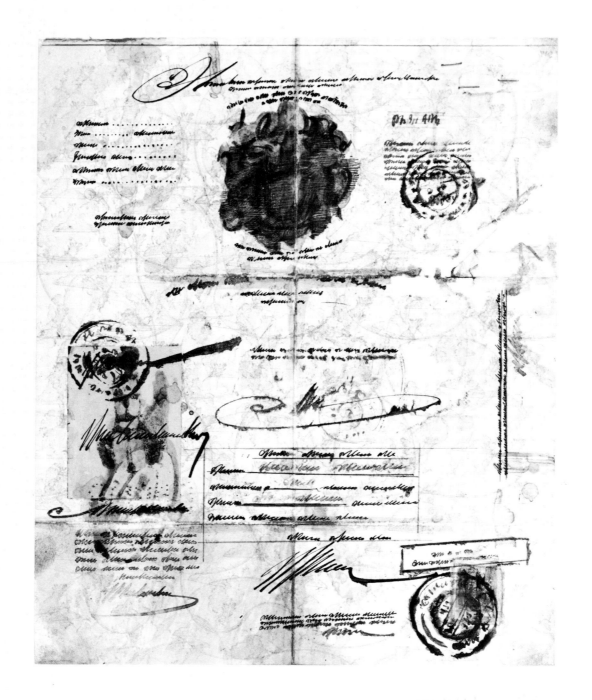

EARLY DOCUMENT, 1952.

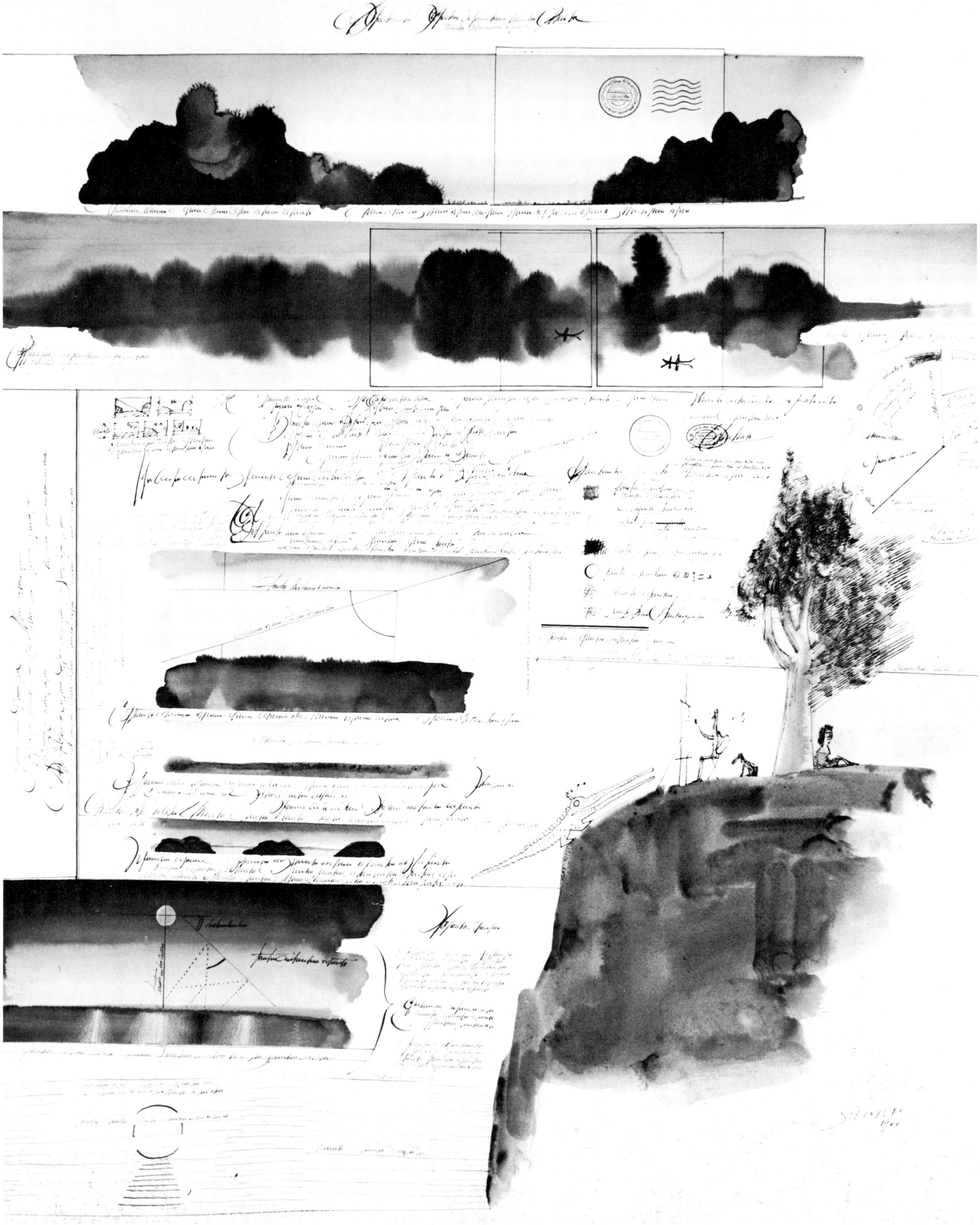

ART (COVER B AND COVER C), 1962.

EVOLUTION, 1967.

ALBERGO MINERVA, 1965.

EXHIBIT TILES, 1973 *(detail)*.

(Facing Page)

LOUSE POINT, 1969.

RAMNICUL SARAT, 1967.

STEINBERG 64

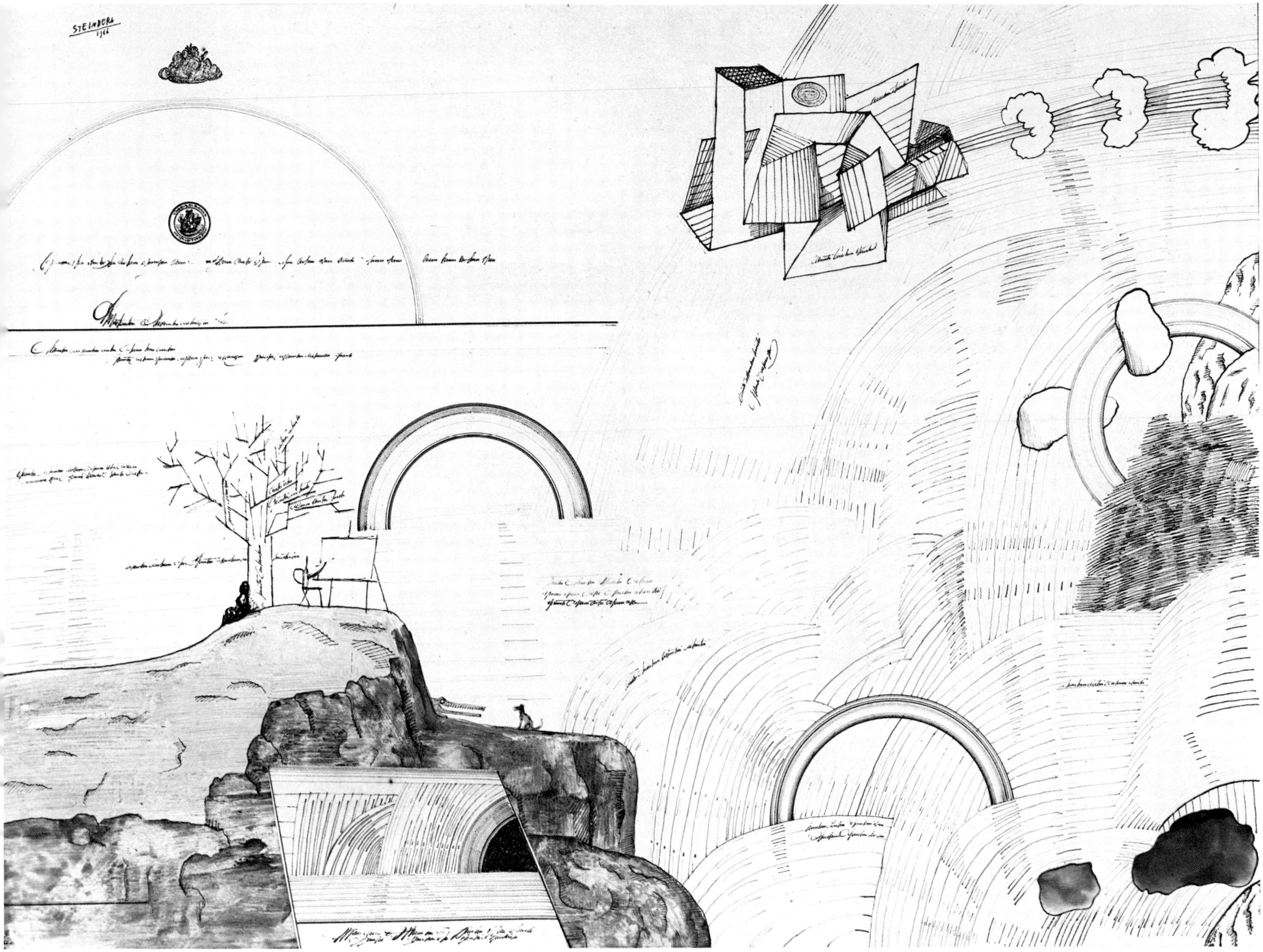

(Facing Page)

RAINBOW LANDSCAPE, 1964.

NIAGARA, 1966.

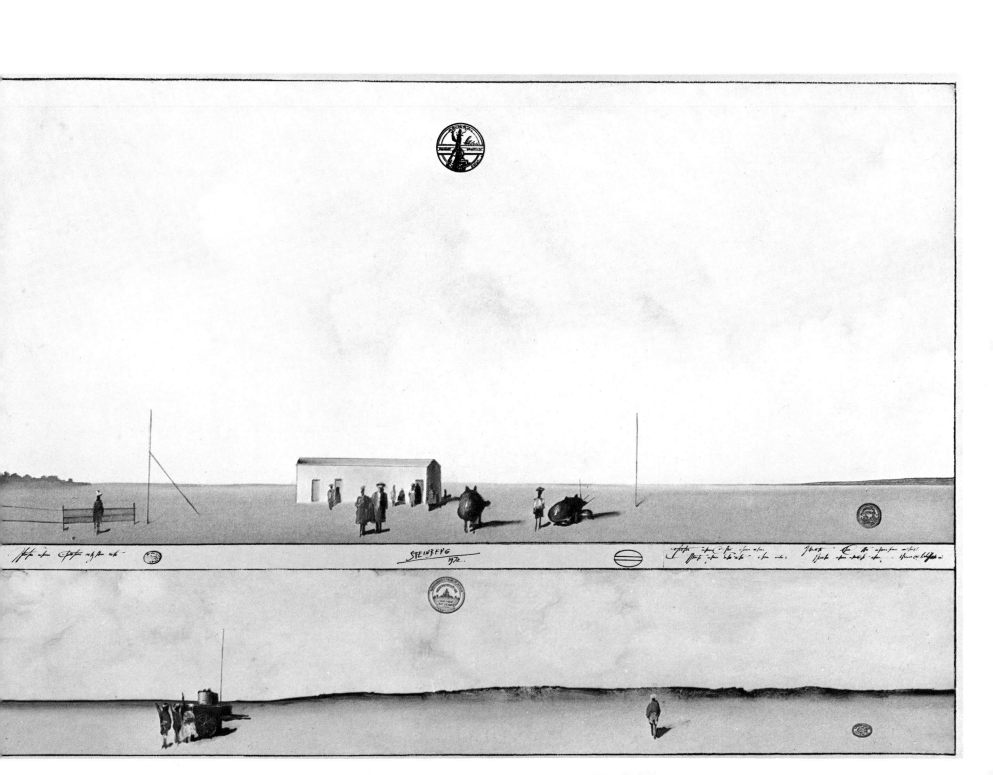

(Facing Page)
UNTITLED, 1973 *(detail).*
ART HISTORY II, 1968.

STEINBERG 1973

STEINBERG 1973

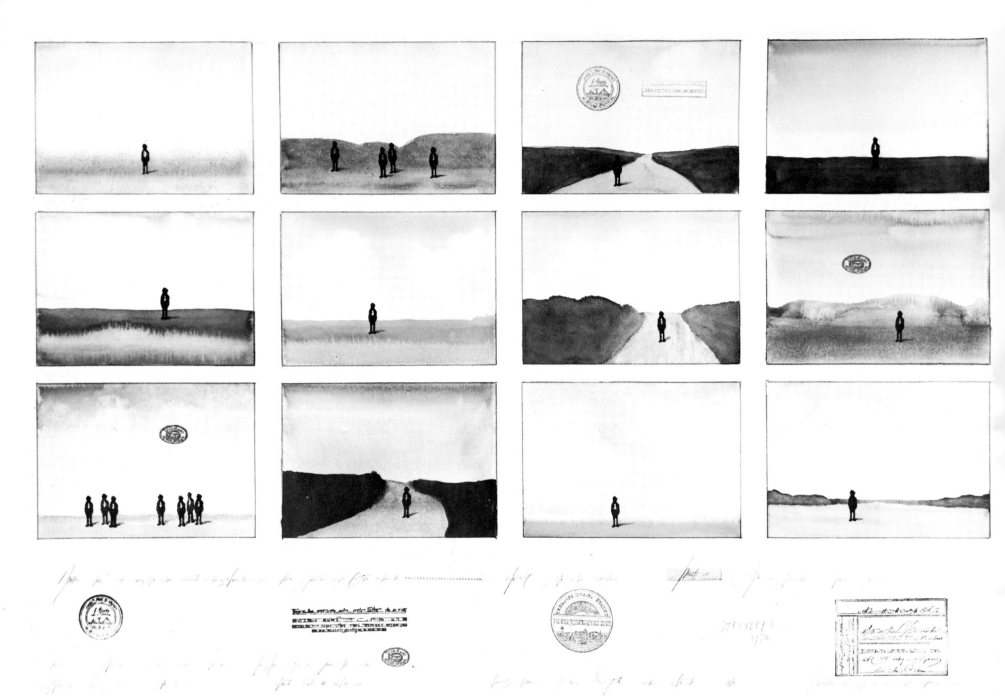

(Preceding Pages)
2 EASTERN SUNSETS, 1973.
2 EASTERN SUNSETS, 1973.
AFRICAN POSTCARDS II, 1972.

BERGAMO, 1966.

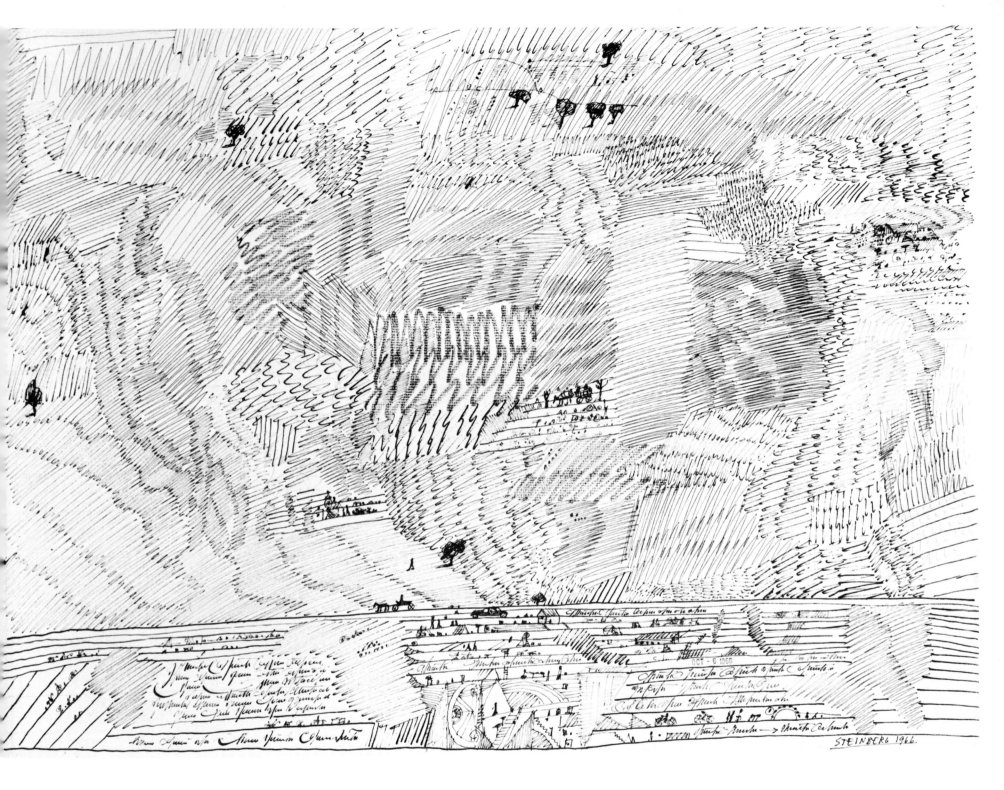

EGYPTIAN LANDSCAPE, 1966.

LAW AND ORDER, 1971.

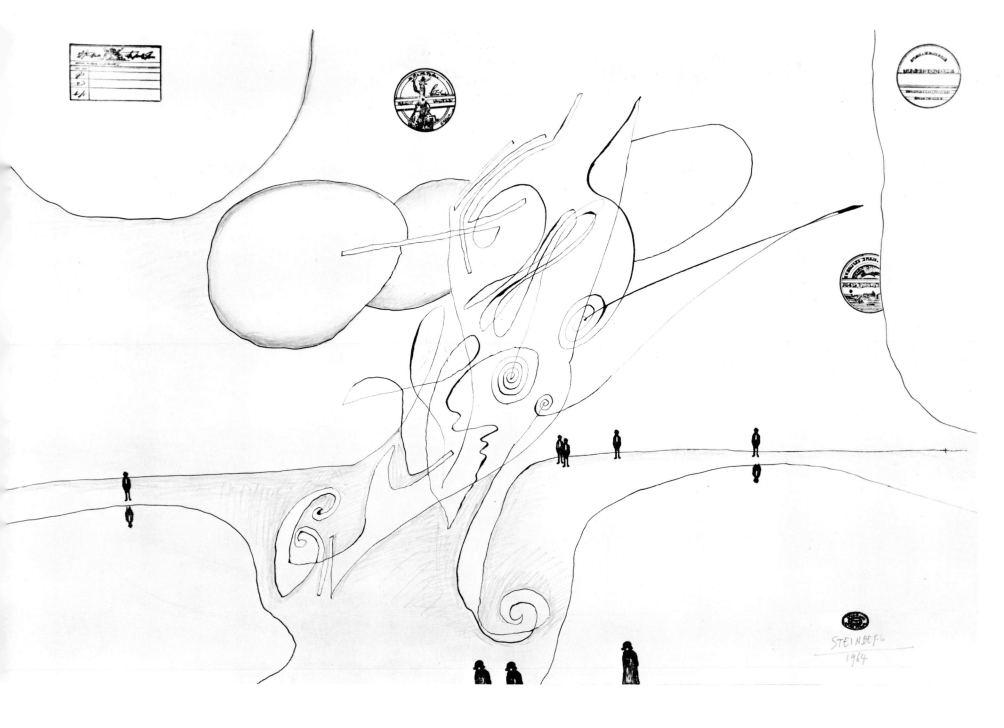

HORIZON, 1964.

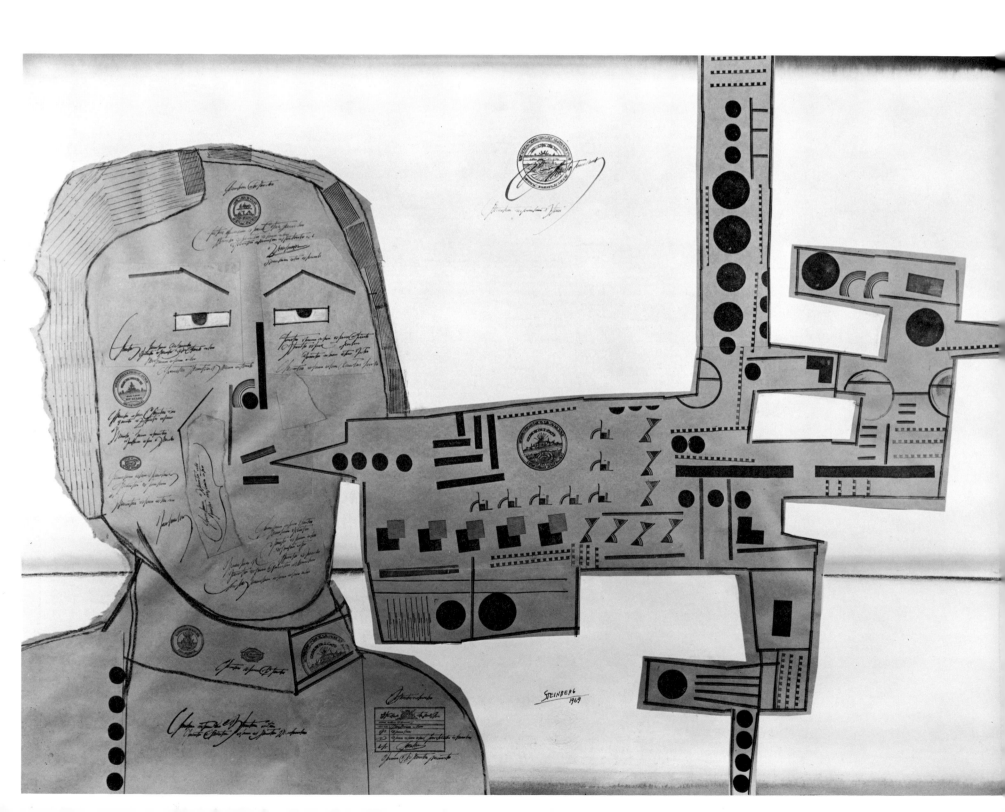

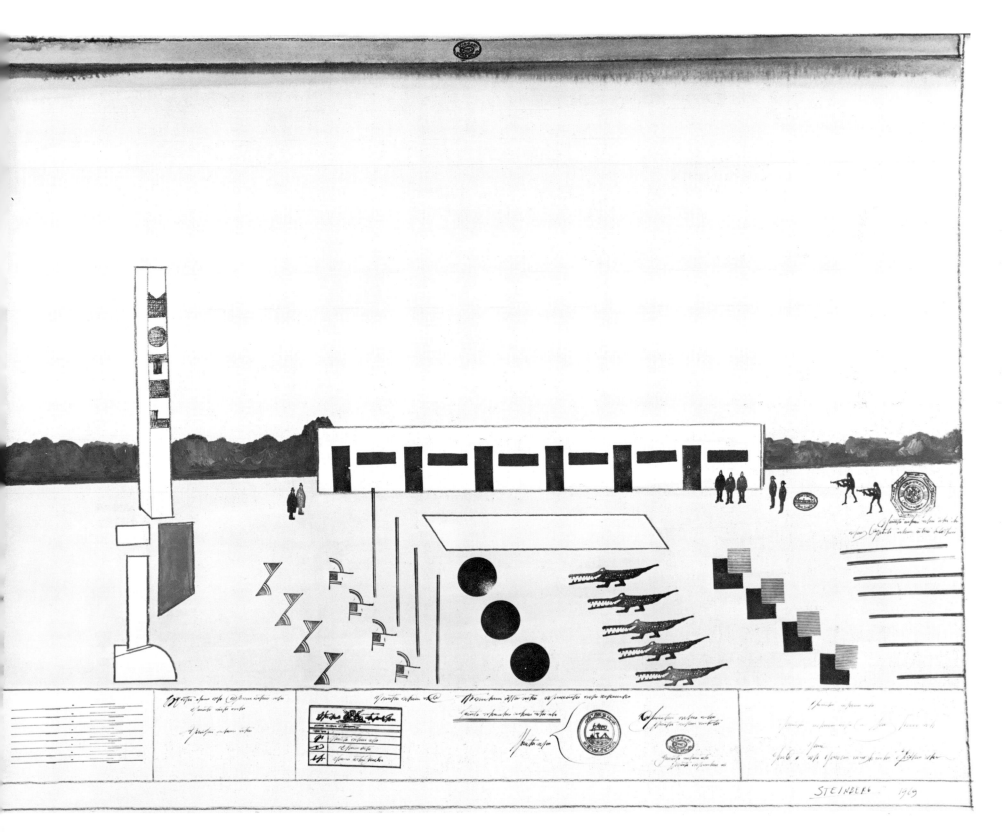

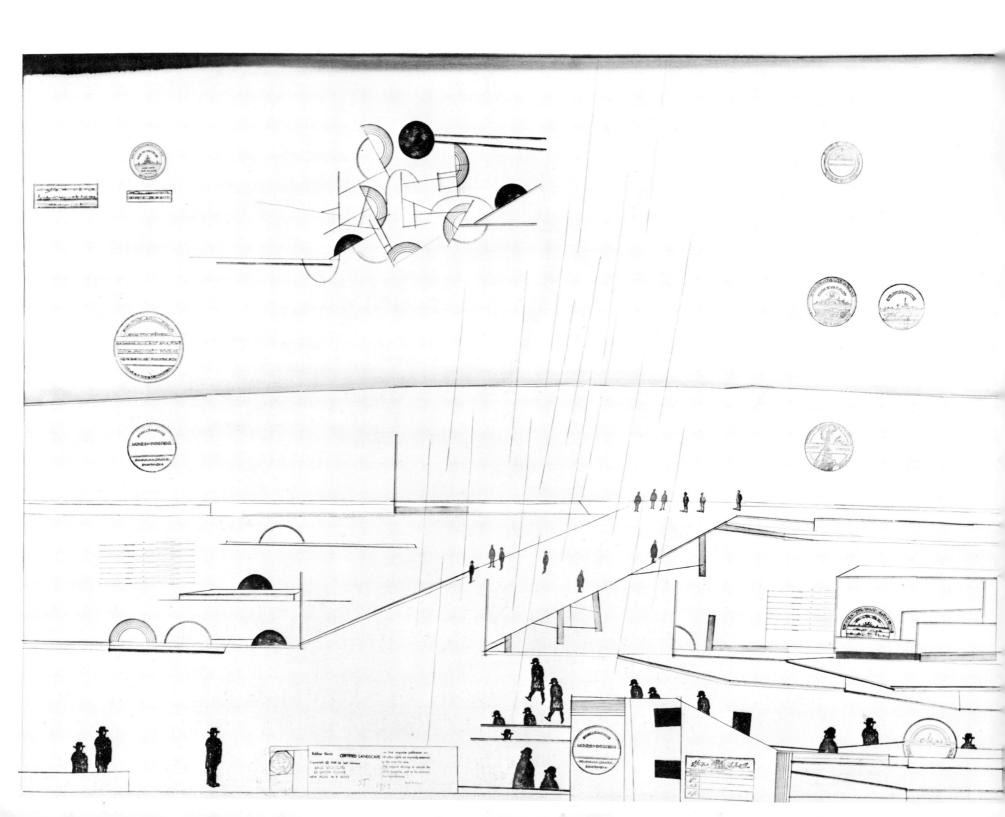

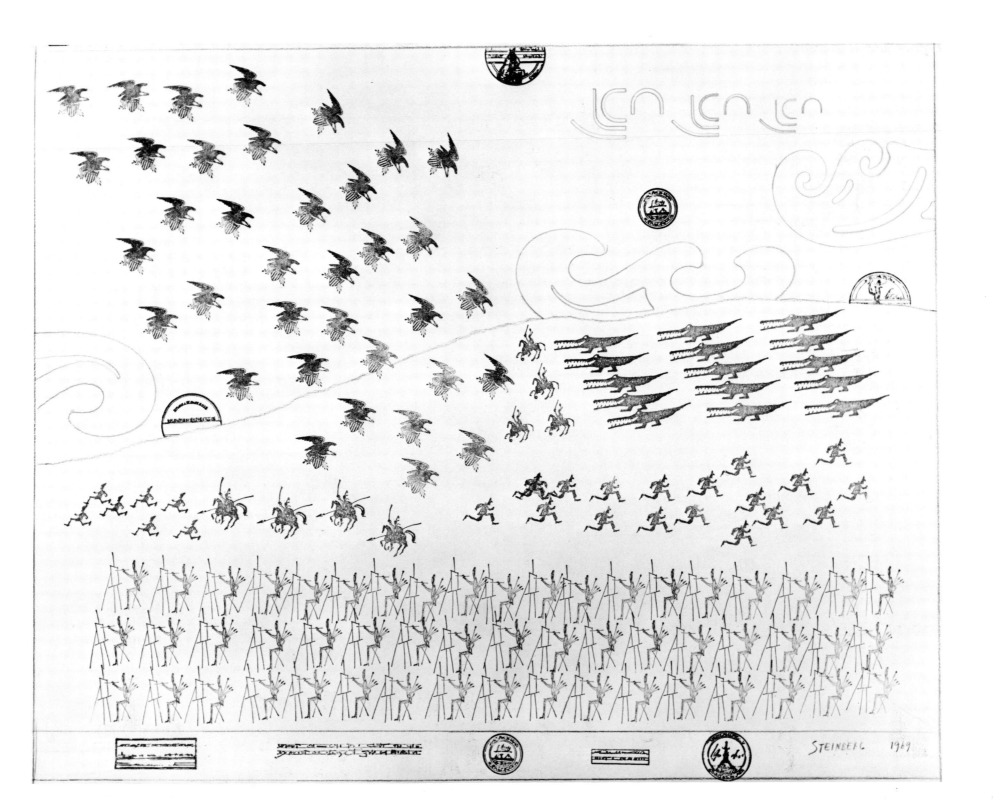

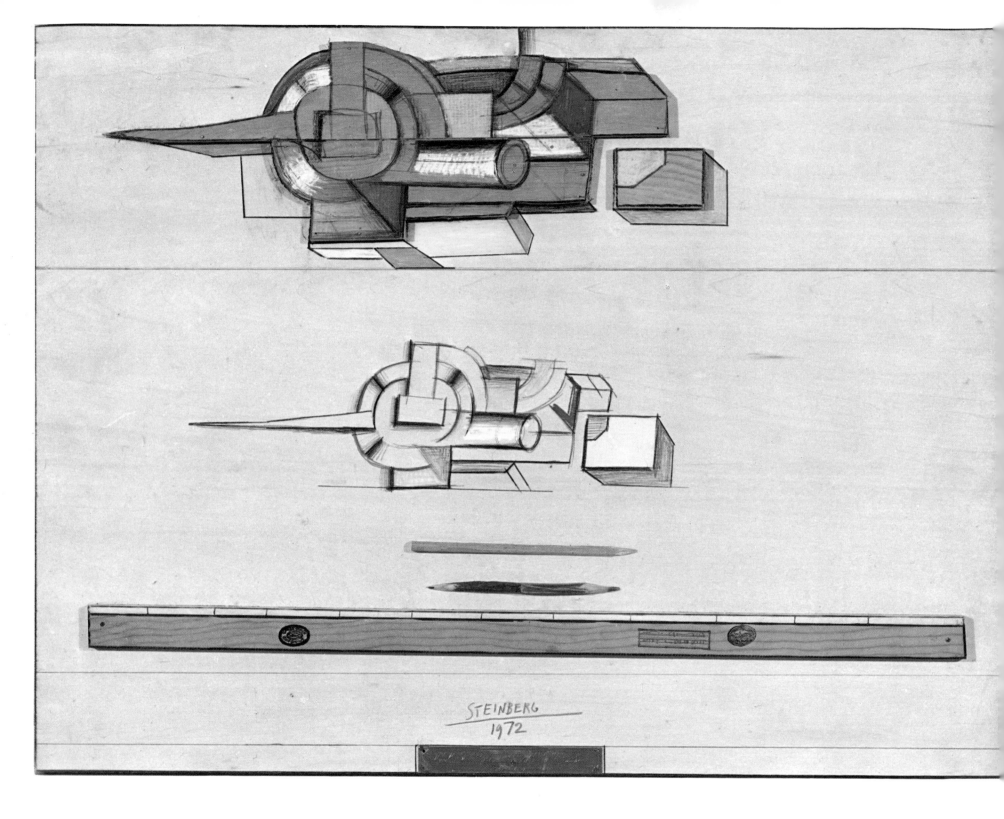

STEINBERG
1972

SPEECH TABLE, 1972.

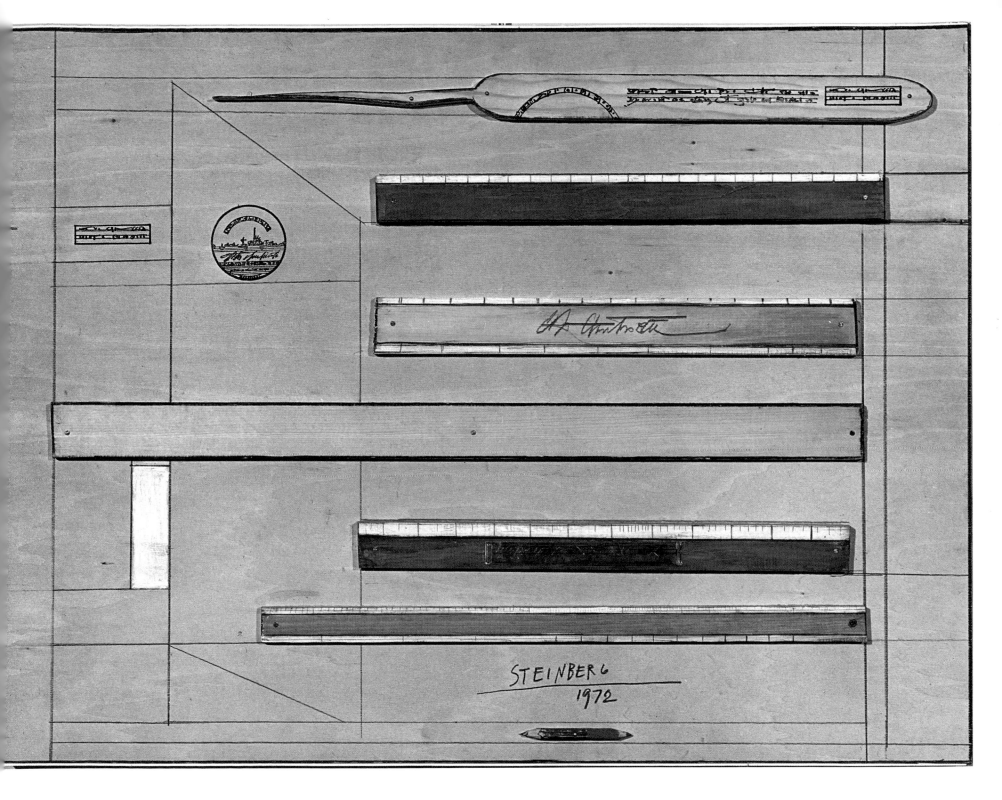

STEINBERG
1972

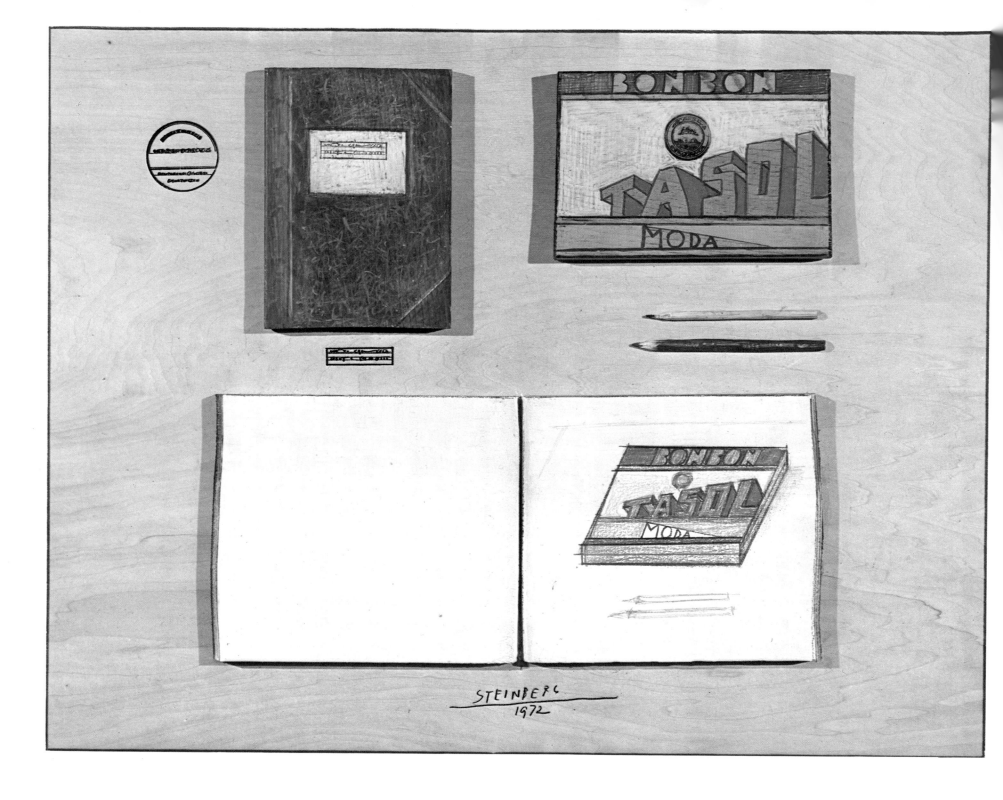

TASOL, 1972.

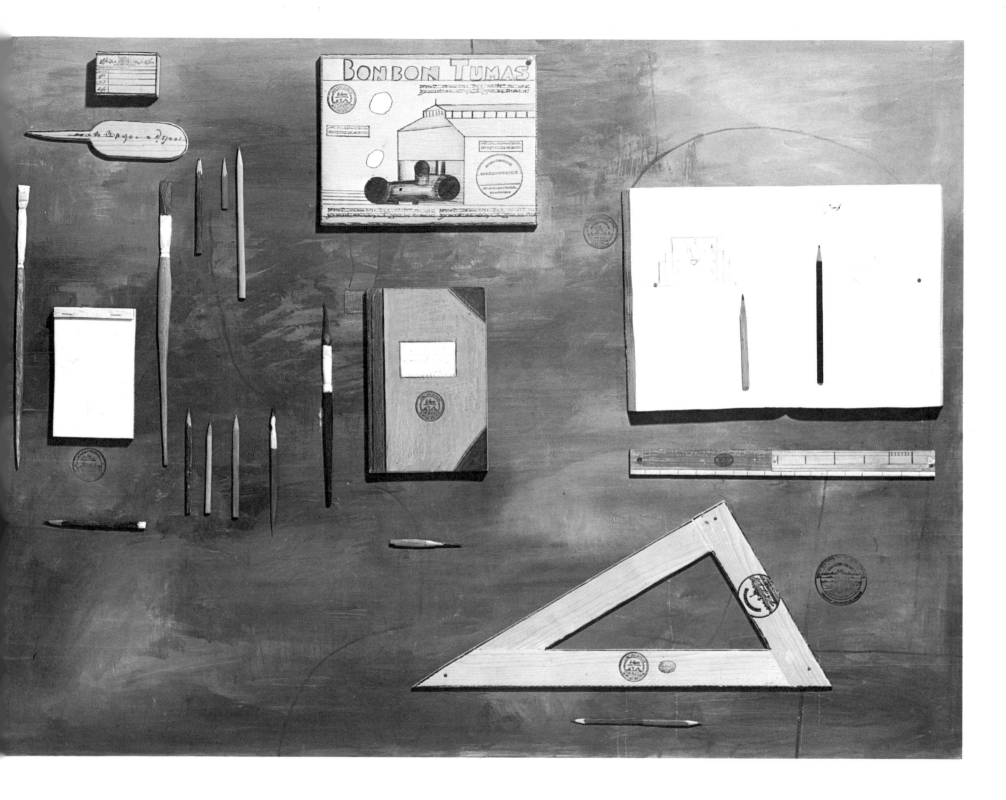

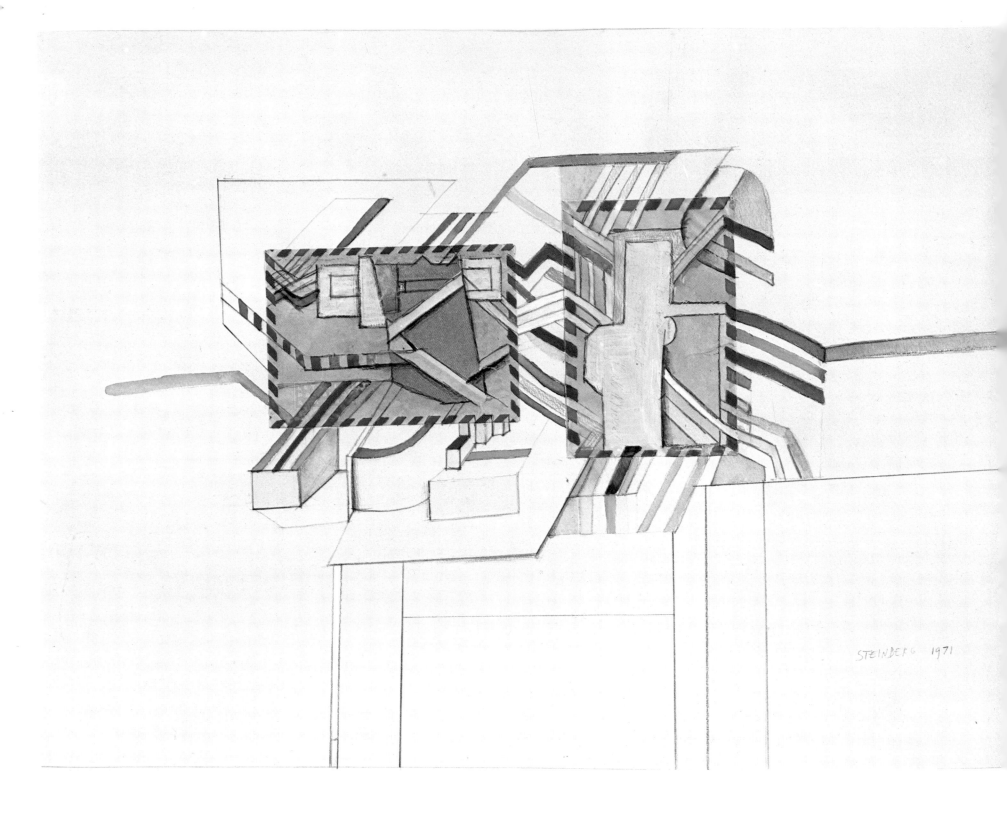

AIR MAIL TABLE, 1971.

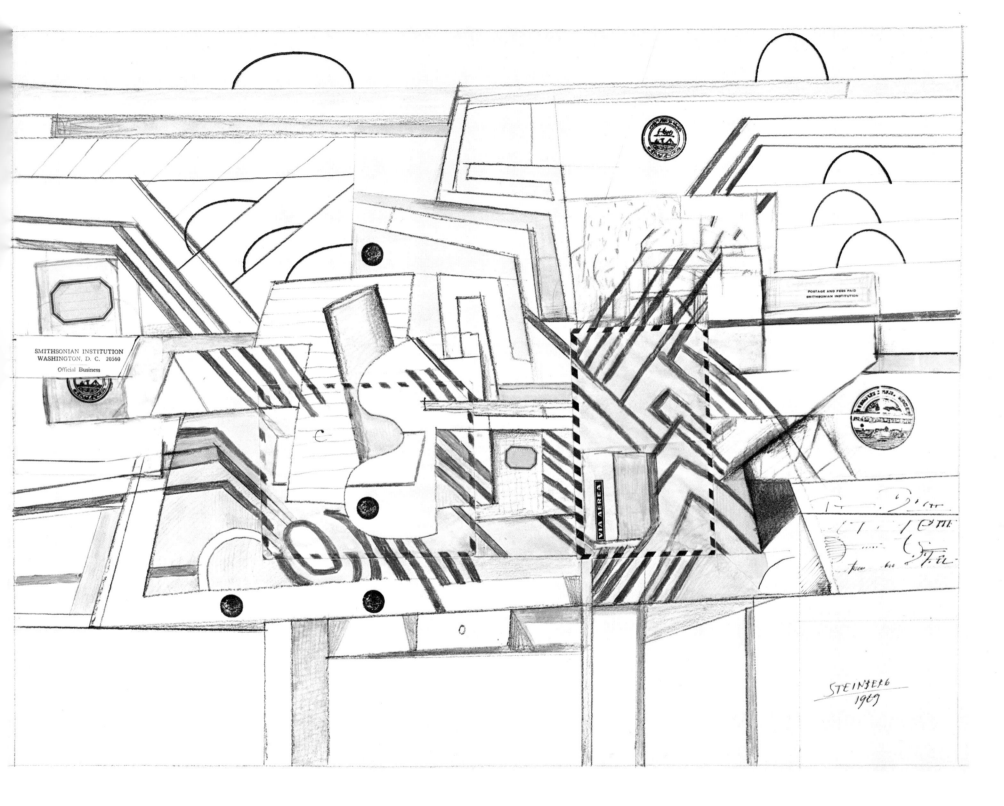

VIA AEREA, 1969.

STEINBERG 1973

TURKISH BOTTLE STILL LIFE, 1973.

RODOZAHARI WATERCOLOR, 1974.

KIBRIT STILL LIFE, 1974.
NUTHATCH STILL LIFE, 1974.
(Overleaf)

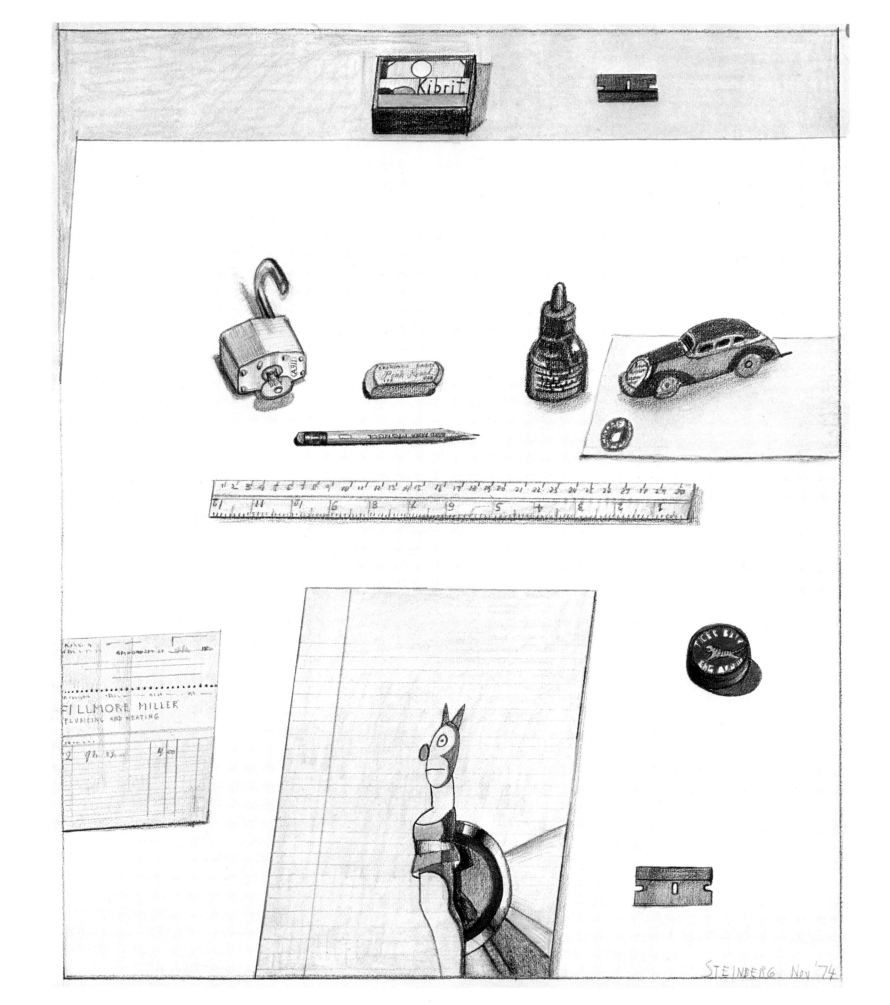

STEINBERG · NOV '74

STEINBERG 1973

16 POSTCARDS, 1973.

16 HORIZONS, 1972.

SPANISH WOMAN, 1966.
BAUHAUS MASK, 1966.
(Overleaf)

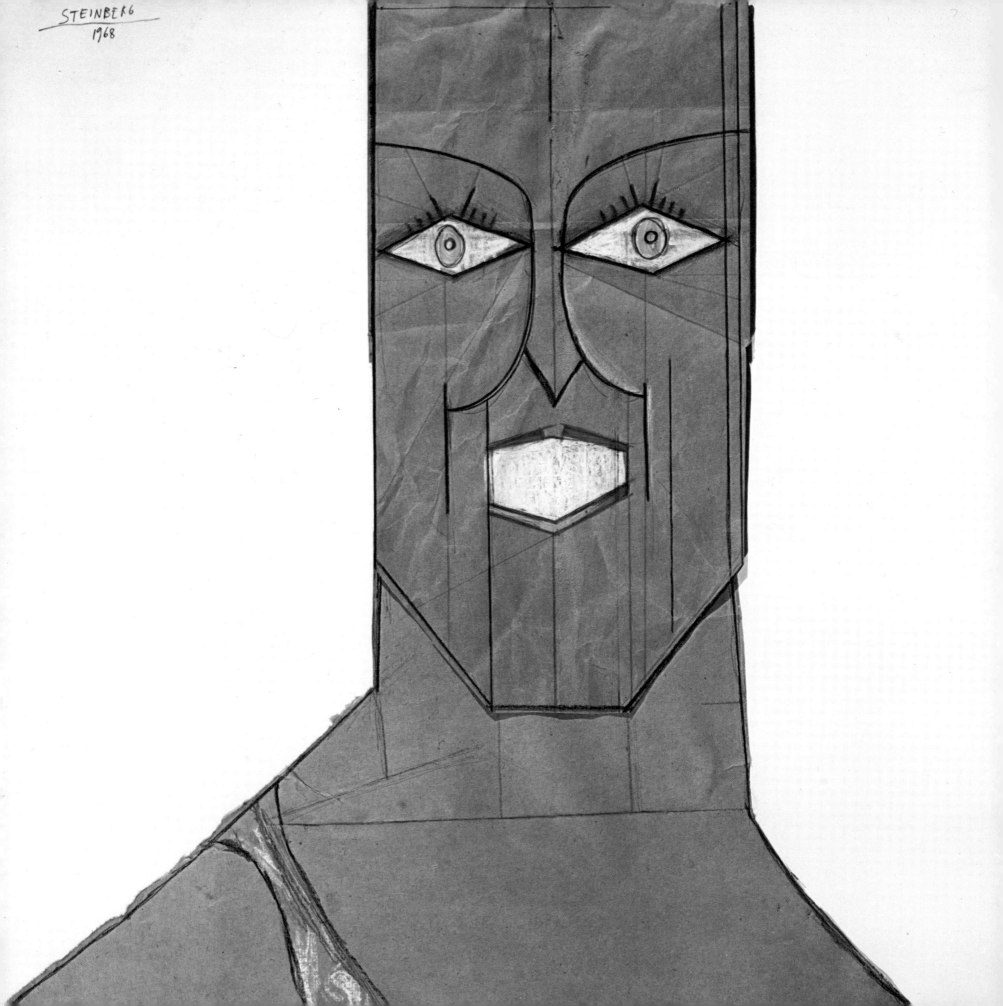

STEINBERG
1968

(Facing Page)

HOSTESS MASK, 1968.

PORTRAIT, 1968.

STEINBERG 68

STEINBERG

MILANO BAUHAUS, 1970.

LAMBRATE, 1971.

WAITING ROOM, 1972.

PENCIL SPIRAL, 1965.

STEINBERG
1966

WOMAN AND TABLE, 1968.

CACOGRAPHER, 1968.

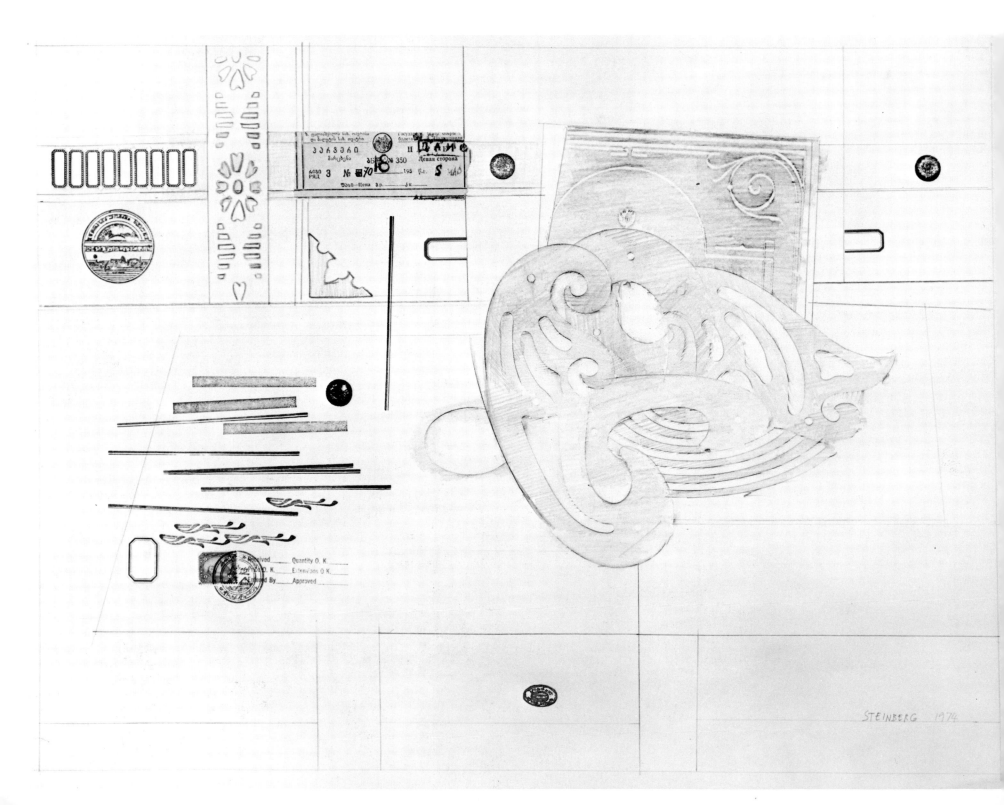

DRAWING TABLE, 1966.

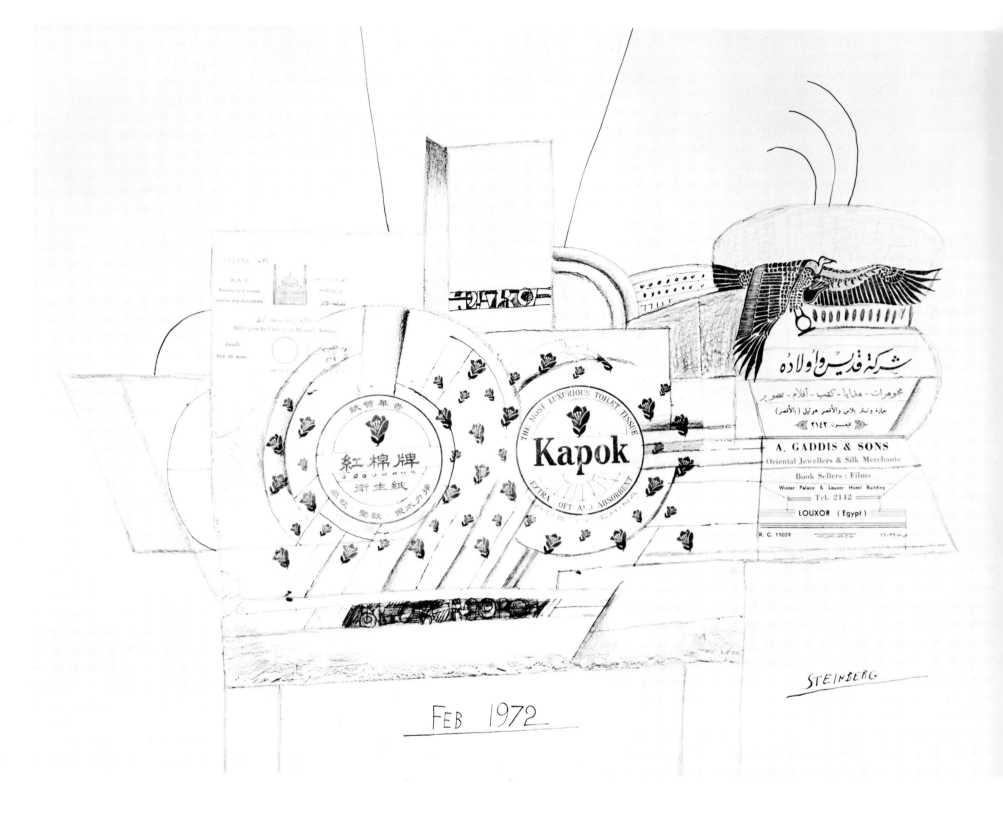

FEB 1972

EGYPT STILL LIFE, 1972.
CADAVRE EXQUIS, 1972.
(Facing Page)

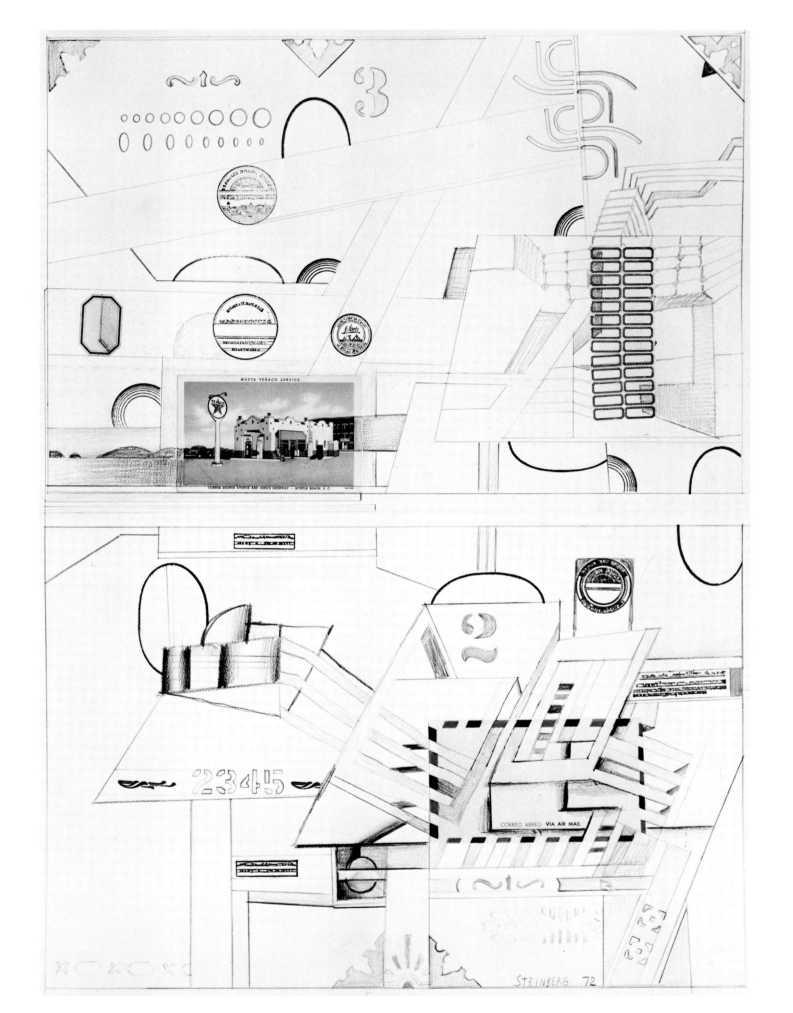

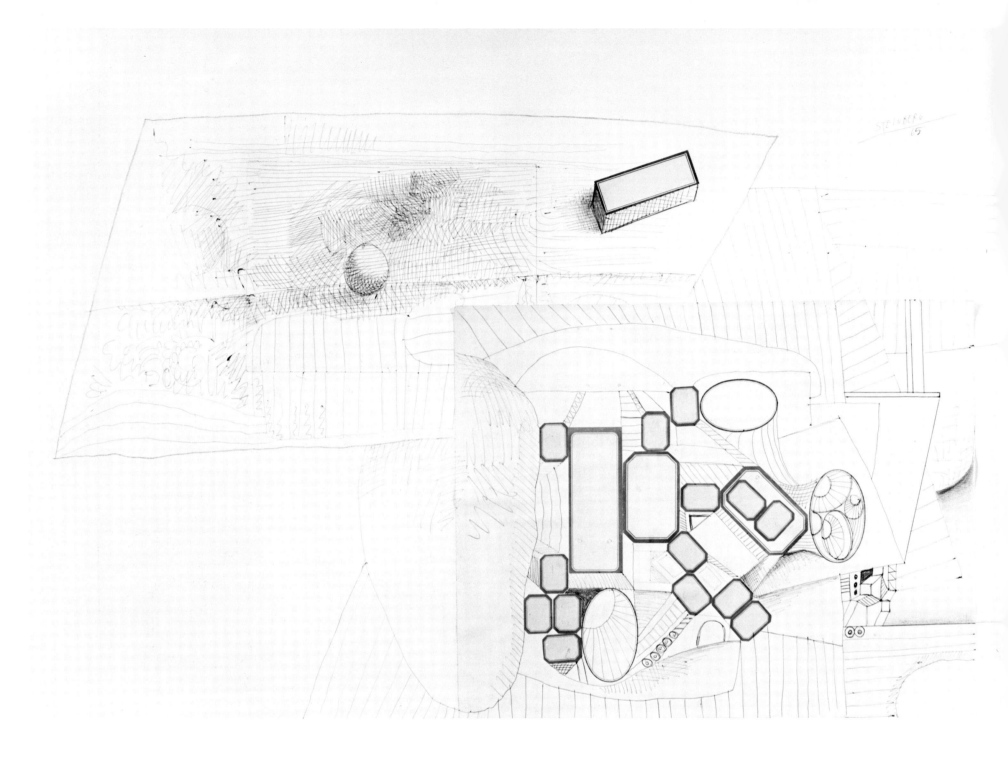

STILL LIFE WITH LABELS, 1965.

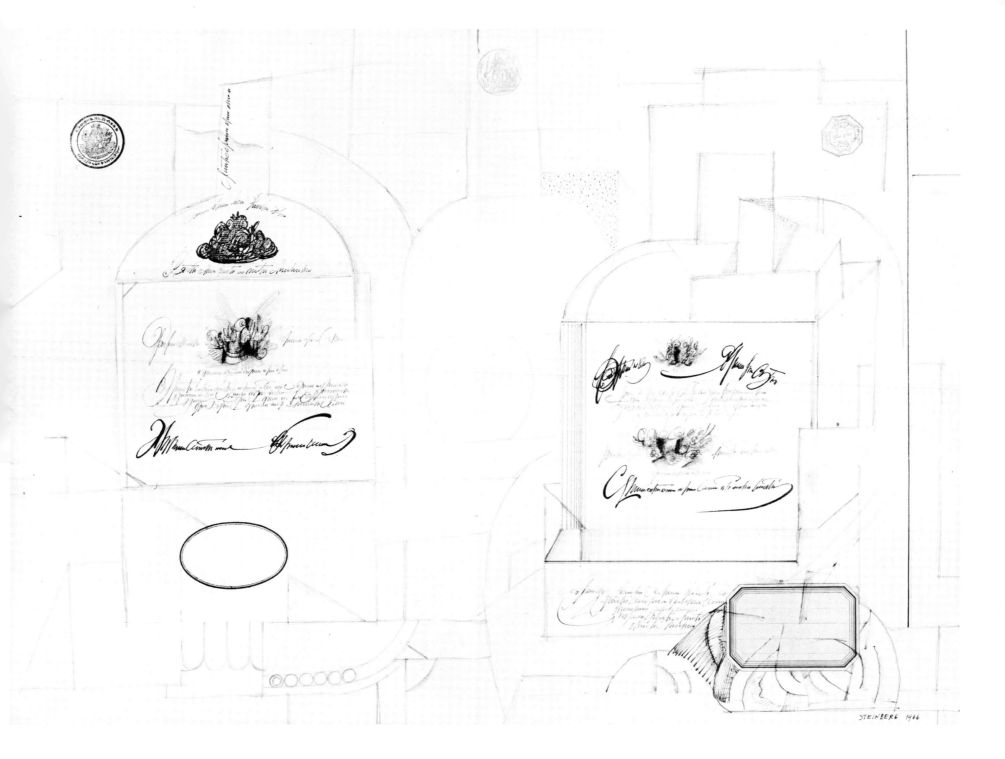

OFFICIAL STILL LIFE, 1966.

STEINBERG STILL LIFE, 1969.
AIR MAIL STILL LIFE, 1971.
CUBISTERIE, 1969.
AIR MAIL TOKYO, 1972.

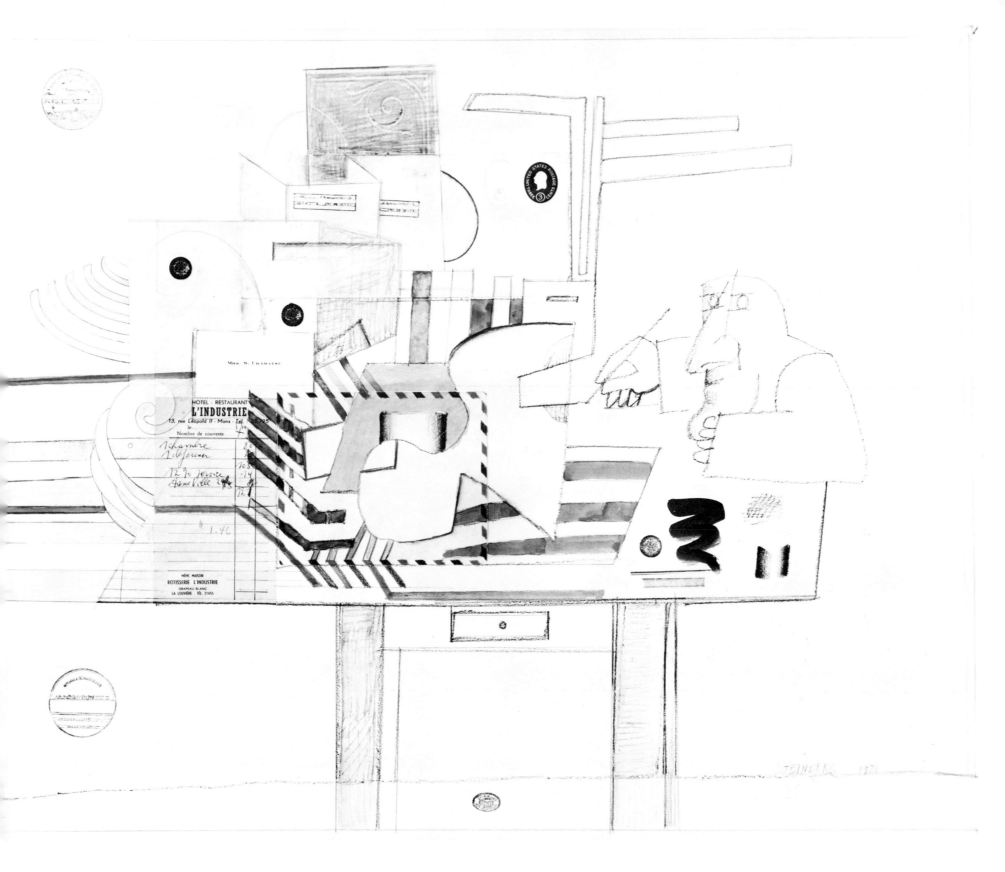

BELGIAN AIR MAIL. 1971.

209

CONGO (MERCENARY MASK), 1966.

STEINBERG 1973

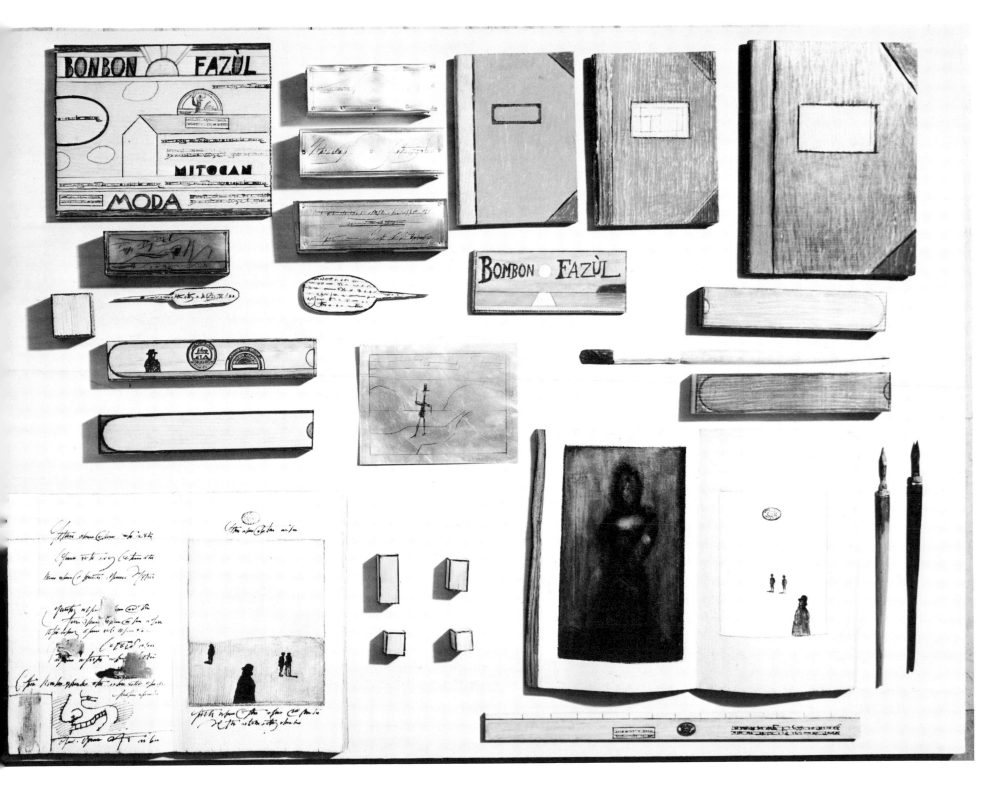

(Facing Page)
COLLECTOR'S TABLE, 1973.

BONBON FAZUL, 1972.

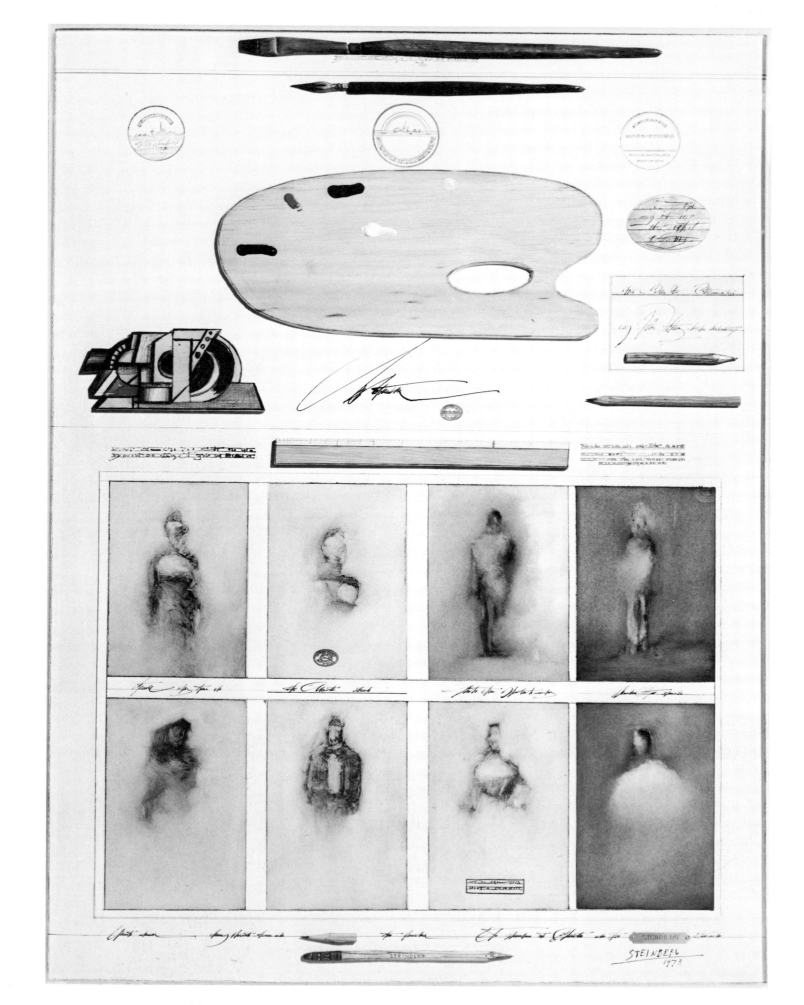

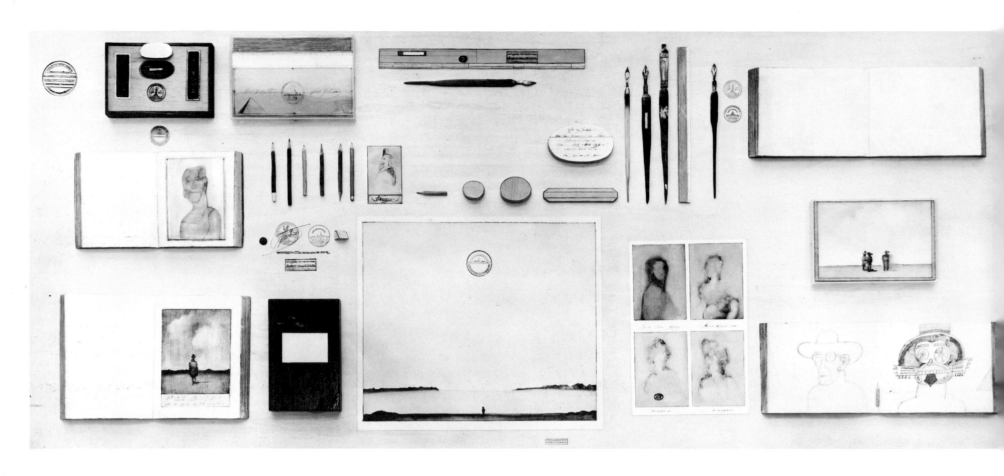

218   GIANT TABLE III, 1971.

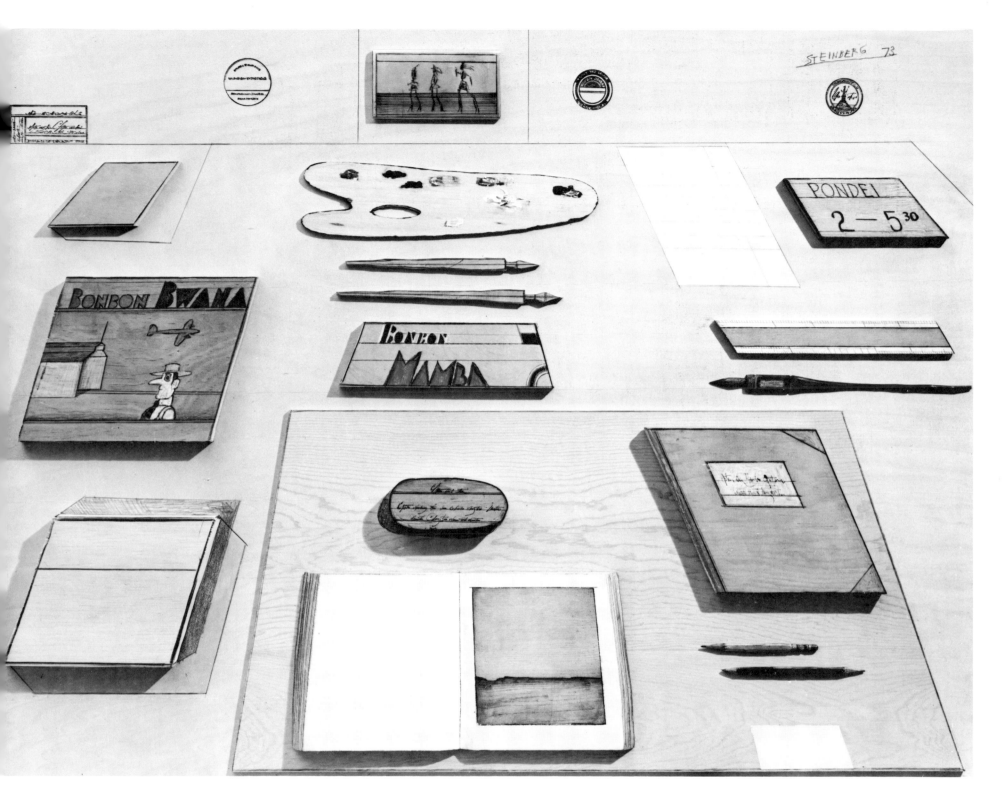

PERSPECTIVE TABLE, 1973.

BONBON PAPUS, 1972.

(Overleaf)

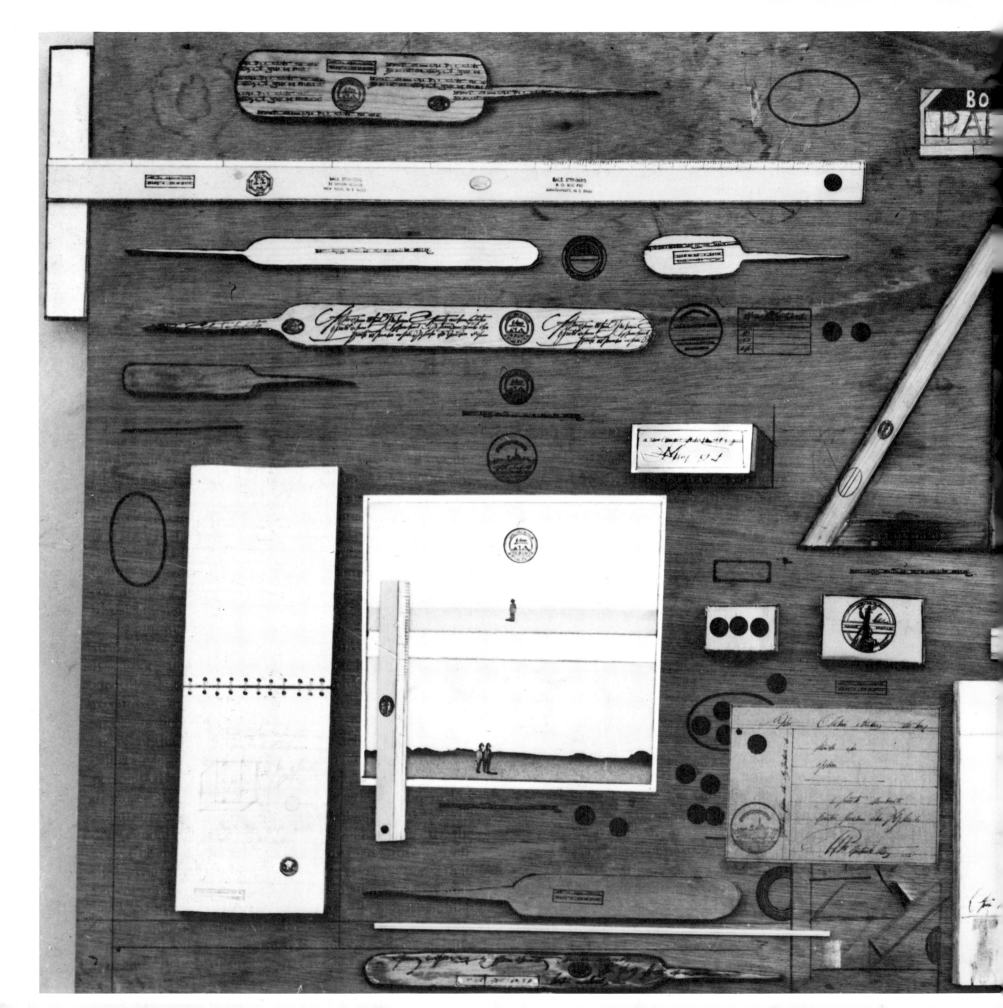

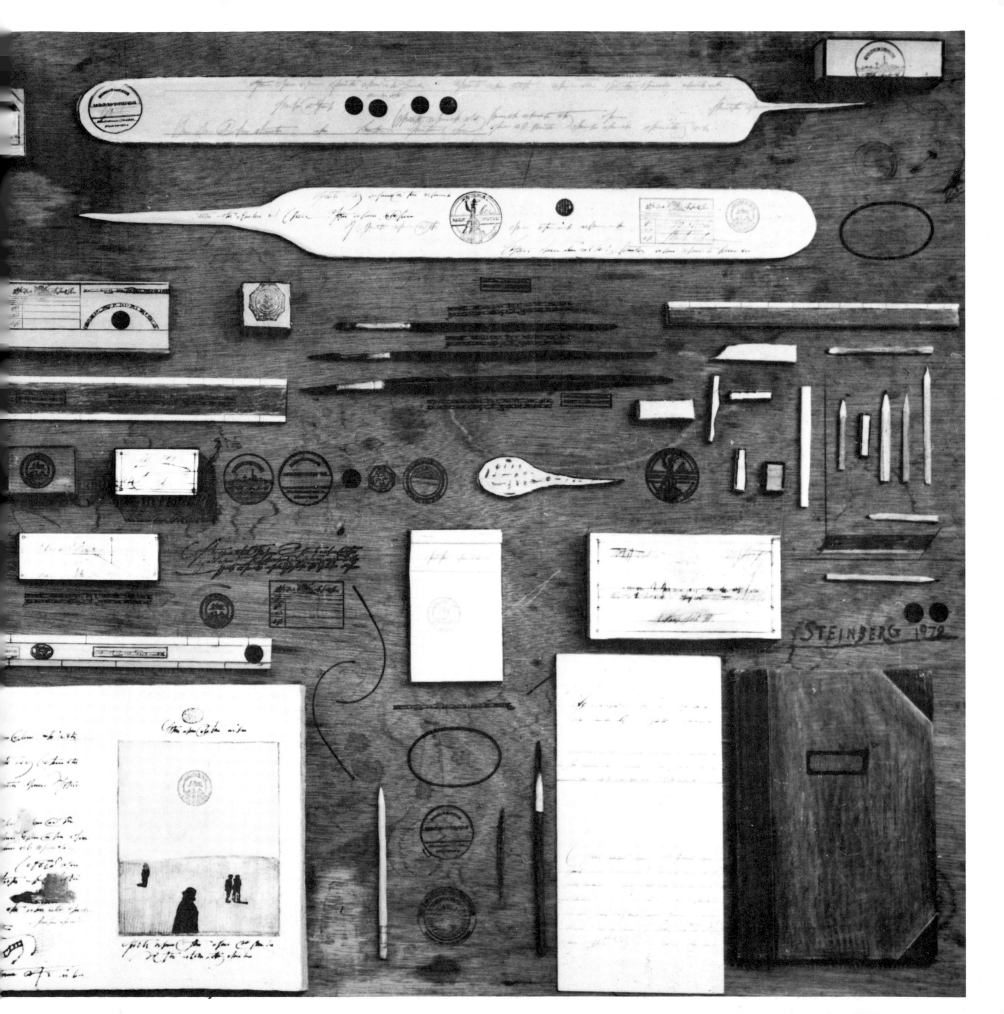

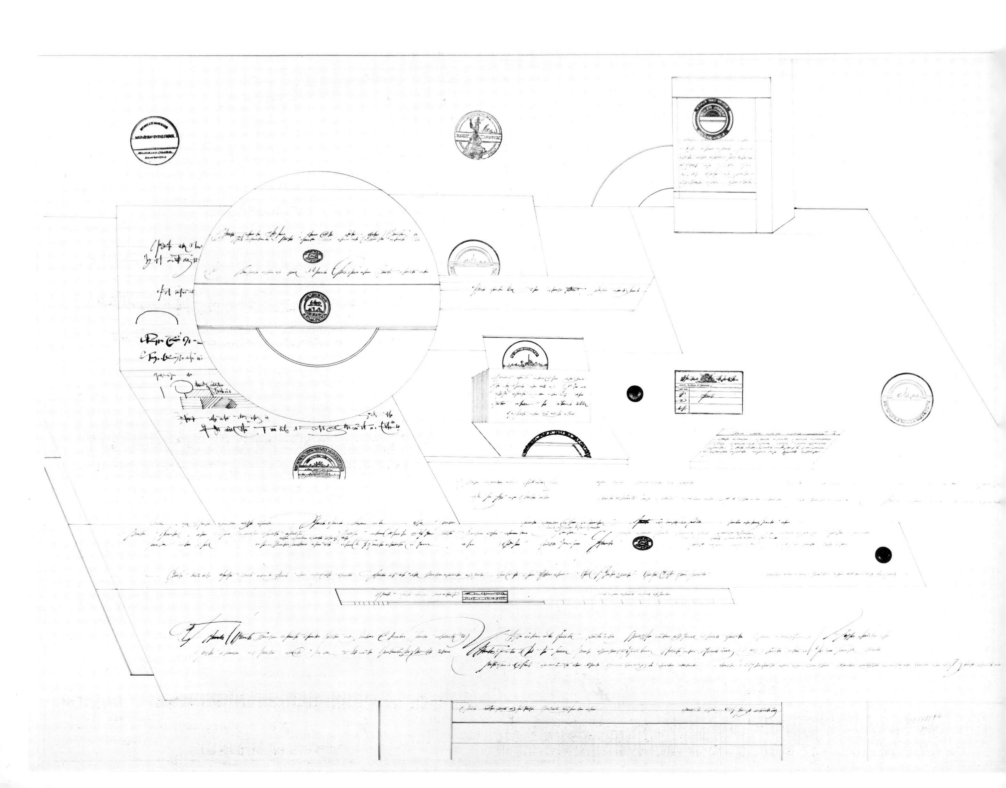

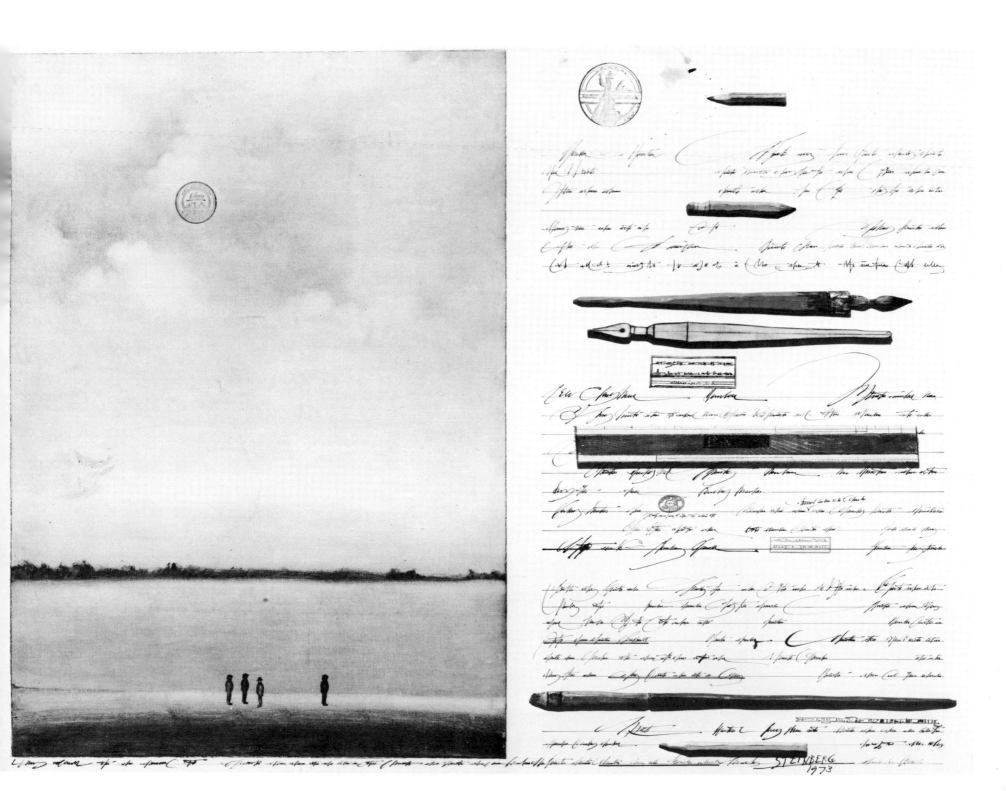

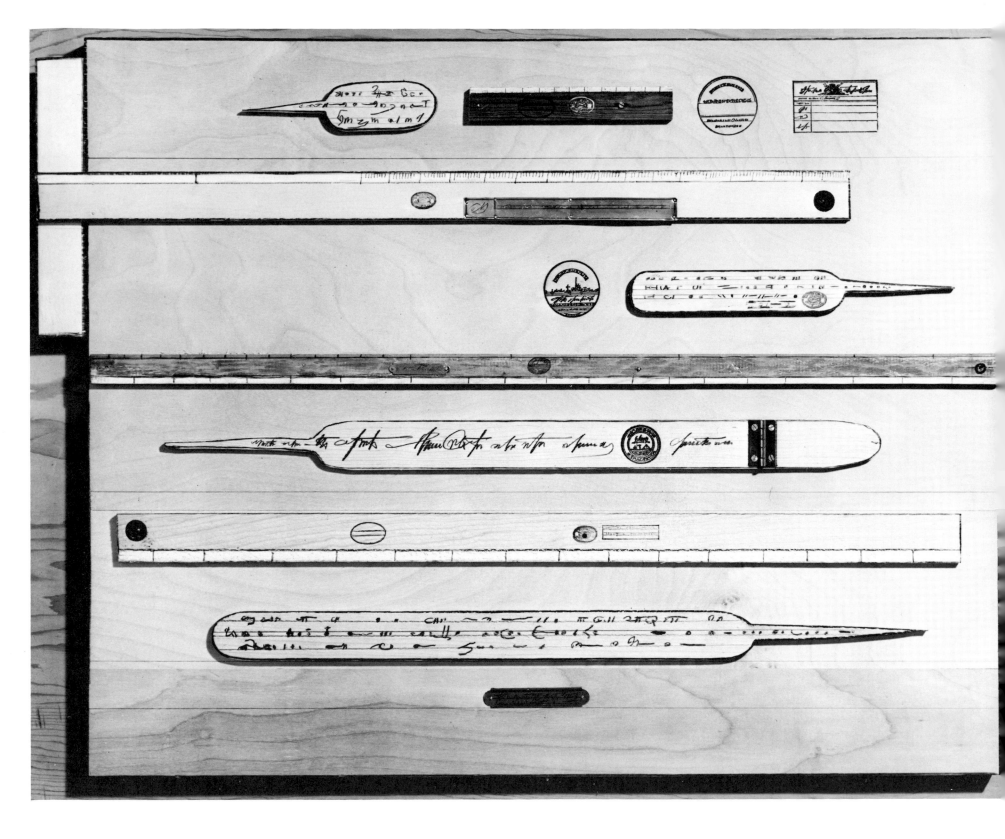

T SQUARE, 1972.

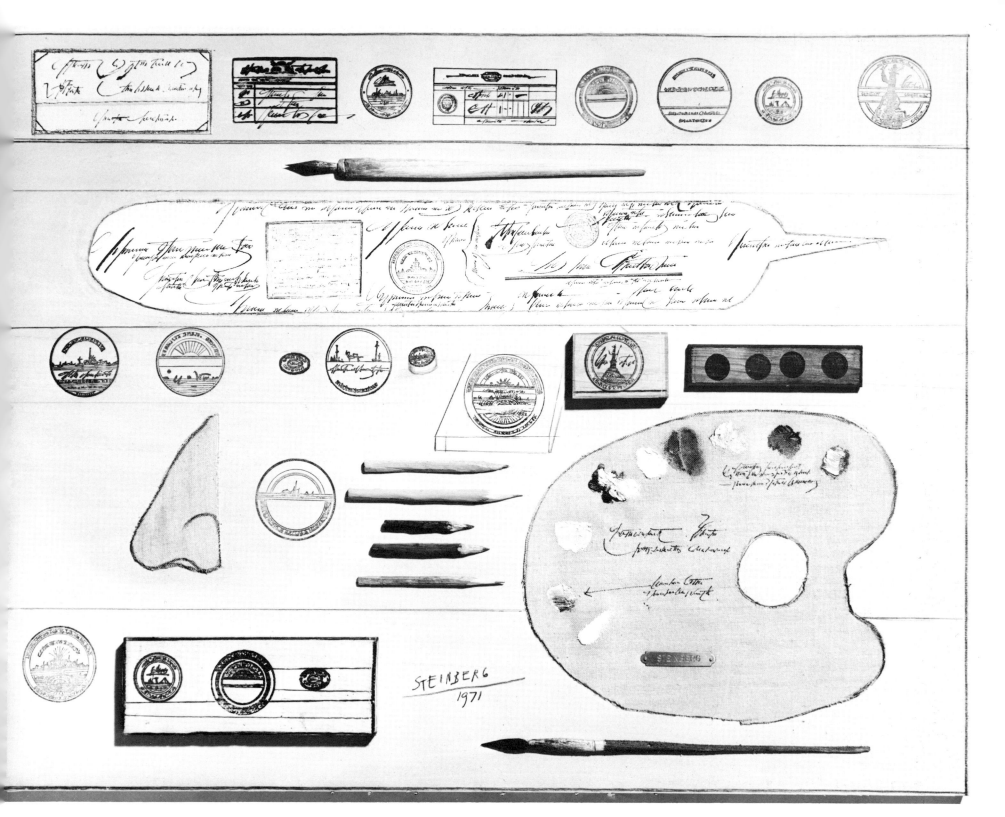

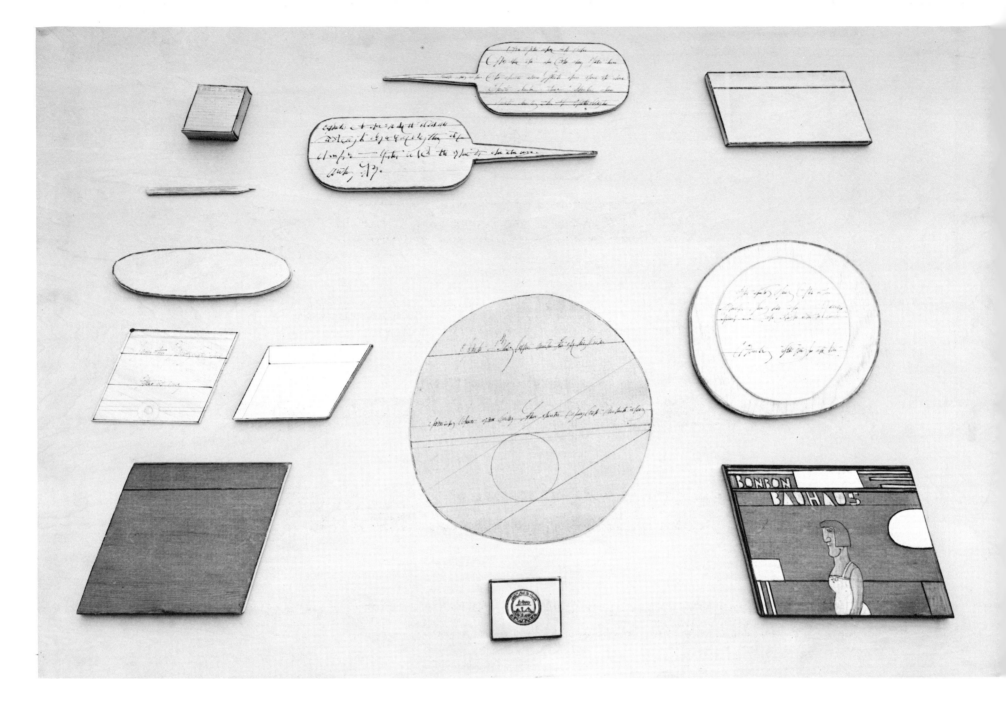

RECORD TABLE, 1972.

RULERS, 1973.

(Facing Page)

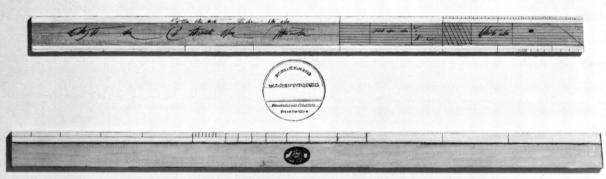

STEINBERG
1973

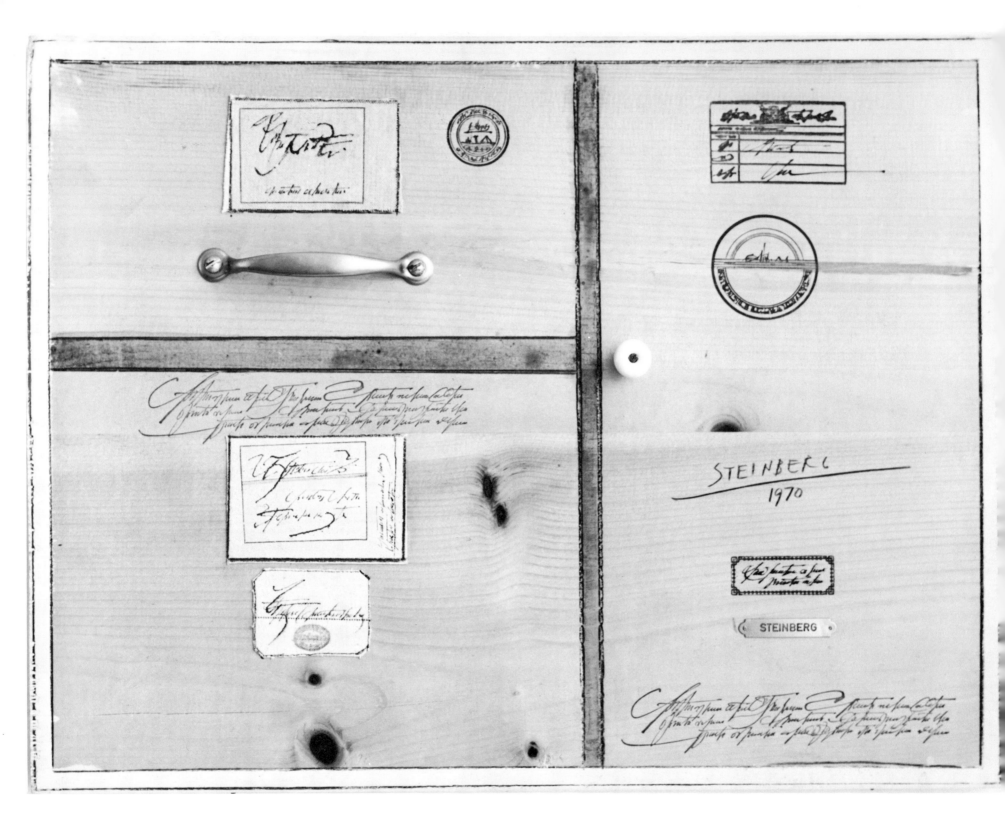

STEINBERG
1970

STEINBERG

CABINET, 1970.

EARLY WORKS, 1969.

List of Plates

Unless otherwise indicated, all works are in the collection of the artist or the Sidney Janis Gallery, New York.

June 15. Born in Ramnicul-Sarat, a small town in southeast Romania. The family moved to Bucharest six months later. The father, Moritz, was a printer and bookbinder, and later a manufacturer of cardboard boxes.

Mother, Rosa Iacobson.

1914

Sister Lica, to whom I remained deeply attached. She was a painter known as Lica Roman and died in Paris in 1975.

MOTHER AND FATHER, 1912

WITH LICA, 1920

After elementary school, entered the Liceul Matei Basarab, an overcrowded, tough school, devoted mostly to Latin.

Spent summers in Buzau, a town near Bucharest, where his grandfather was a military tailor.

1924

Graduated from high school and entered the University of Bucharest, frequenting the courses of Philosophy and Letters.

1932

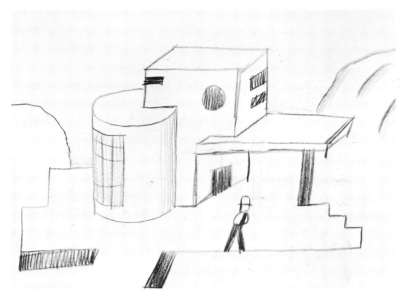

To Milan, Italy, where enrolled in the Politecnico, Facoltà di Architettura, a comfortable school that was under the influence of Cubism, and where one learned mostly from schoolmates.

The class traveled to Ferrara and Rome, on a field trip that remains an important and happy memory.

Returned to Romania for the summer vacations by tramp steamer from Genoa to Naples, Catania, Piraeus, several Greek islands, Istanbul and Constanza.

Started publishing cartoons for *Bertoldo*, a biweekly printed in Milan.

From *Bertoldo, 1936*

— Accidenti, questo non sono io. Con tutta quella gente che era per la strada mi sono perso.

"Dammit, this isn't me! I got lost in the crowd."

1933 *The study of architecture is a marvelous training for anything but architecture. The frightening thought that what you draw may become a building makes for reasoned lines.*

1934 *It was the first time I drew from life — in Italian, dal vero, "from the true." In fact, one has to tell the truth in*

1935 *order to make a good drawing, a poetic invention of the moment, a truth that demands the elimination of all our talent (ready-made vocabulary). It demands genuine clumsiness. In fact, the best clumsy ones are Cézanne and*

1936 *Matisse.*

In Fascist Italy, where the controlled press was predictable and extremely boring, the humor magazines were a way of knowing other aspects of life, which, by the nature of humor itself, seemed subversive.

This is one of the first drawings for Bertoldo (and in the avant-garde of the identity problem).

I am among the few who continue to draw after childhood is ended, continuing and perfecting childhood drawing — without the traditional interruption of academic training.

The continuous line of my drawing dates from childhood and is probably a way of writing from my illiterate days.

235

His drawings were published in *Life* magazine and *Harper's Bazaar*.

Graduated as Dottore in Architettura.

1940

Left Italy via Lisbon and New York (Ellis Island) for Santo Domingo.

Started publishing regularly in *The New Yorker* and the newspaper *PM*.

1941

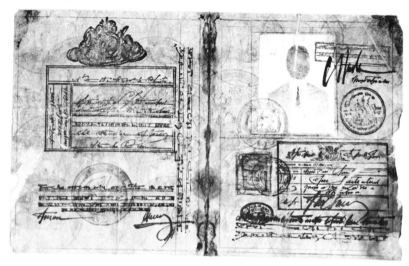

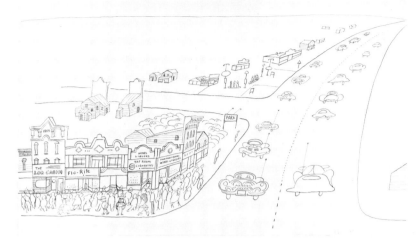

The view from the car is false, menacing; one is seated too low, as if in a living-room chair watching TV in the middle of a highway. From the bus, one has a much better and nobler view, the view of the horseman. It is a pity that now they color the bus windows and one sees only a sad, permanent twilight.

In July to United States as an immigrant, landing in Miami and continuing by bus to New York (the first of many trips by bus around the country).

To Chicago and Los Angeles, returning via Arizona, Texas, etc., by train.

Enlisted in the Navy.

1942

Commissioned as an ensign in the USNR and became a United States citizen. Stationed in Washington.

First show at Betty Parsons.

1943

CALCUTTA

Sent overseas to Colombo (Ceylon), to Calcutta and to Kunming (China), where he was attached to the Fourteenth Air Force. Traveled to Chungking, Kweilin and Hengyang.

KUNMING

CHINA

INDIA

Transferred to the European theater, via Cairo and Algiers to Italy.

In October returned to the United States. Stationed in Washington, D.C.

1944

ALGERIA

Louis Faurer

MARRIED TO HEDDA STERNE.

ST.

All in Line, a book of wartime drawings of China, India, North Africa and Italy.

1945

Released from the Navy.

As war correspondent for *The New Yorker*, covered the Nuremberg trials.

Lived in Paris.

1946

ITALY

This kitten became a dear personage. I know him only from this photograph — taken in Vermont in 1947 in a house of friends — and I wasn't aware of that cat at the time. How beautiful and elegant he is. He probably made a sidewise jump a moment after the picture was taken.

Traveled to Mexico.   **1947**
Mural for Terrace Plaza Hotel, in Cincinnati.

Art of Living, a book about: CHAIRS, SUBWAYS, TAXIS,   **1949**
SALOONS, SIDEWALKS, DERELICTS, PERSPECTIVE,
BIRDS, CATS, HORSES, ART AND WOMEN.

Made first drawings on objects
— chairs, bathtubs, boxes.

Lived in Hollywood for two months and traveled through   **1950**
California, Nevada, Utah.

I was hired — or, rather, my hand was hired — to play the hand of Gene Kelly drawing and painting in <u>An American in Paris</u>. But Hollywood was not for me. I quarreled with the producer and resigned after one day or less.

It was the first time I had seen a highway city, which was to be the model for the rest of our cities. Los Angeles is the avant-garde city of parody in architecture and even in nature (canyons and palm trees). Difficult to draw, a trap — like portraying clowns.

Lived in Palermo and traveled through southern Italy.   **1951**
Later revisited Milan and Venice.

Had double show at Sidney Janis and Betty Parsons galleries (when these two galleries were on the same floor at 15 East Fifty-seventh Street).

1952

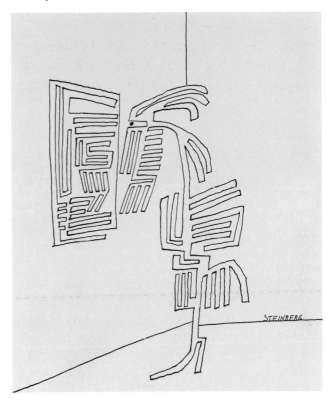

Traveled to South America: Brazil (Rio, São Paulo, Manaus, and the Amazon River) and Argentina.

Showed for the first time in Paris, at the Galerie Maeght.

1953

When traveling, I seldom worked. I loved to arrive in a new place and face the new situations like one newly born who sees life for the first time, when it still has the air of fiction. (It lasts one day.)

There was also a geographical snobbism on my part. To find myself in Manaus seemed to me so extraordinary an achievement as to make me truly famous in my own eyes.

After all these travels, now I hardly go beyond Paris or Bergamo. One mostly travels to airports, visits travel agencies and is surrounded by waiters and tourists.

Pretexts for travel: In the spring I visited the battlefields and headquarters of the Civil War, from Gettysburg to Vicksburg, a perfect way of seeing strange places like Appomattox.

Traveled with the Milwaukee Braves and made a series of baseball drawings for *Life*.

1954

Passport

Passport, a book about: FALSE DOCUMENTS, PASSPORTS, DIPLOMAS, CERTIFICATES, FALSE PHOTOGRAPHS (WITH FALSE AUTOGRAPHS), FALSE ETCHINGS, FALSE WINE LABELS, LETTERS, DIARIES, MANUSCRIPTS, FALSE EX-VOTOS, CALLIGRAPHY AND CACOGRAPHY.
FINGERPRINTS, PARADES, COCKTAIL PARTIES, BALLET, BILLIARDS, COWBOYS, PITCHERS, PALM TREES, CATS, DOG WALKERS, HORSEWOMEN, GUITAR PLAYERS, AUTOMOBILES, LOCOMOTIVES, RAILWAY STATIONS, BRIDGES, SUMMER AND WINTER, FASHIONS, SPHINXES.
VICTORIAN ARCHITECTURE, ART NOUVEAU, RUBBER-STAMP ARCHITECTURE, SLUMS, SKYSCRAPERS.
TRAVEL NOTES FROM WESTERN EUROPE, MIDDLE EAST, MIDDLE WEST, PALM BEACH, ISTANBUL, MANAUS AND HOLLYWOOD.

Lived in Paris, published *Dessins*.

1955

In summer I traveled with the Milwaukee Braves to National League towns like Philadelphia, Cincinnati, Chicago, Milwaukee and Brooklyn — an excellent pretext for visiting unattractive parts of town and the hotels where the sports people live. And an opportunity for learning as much as possible about the game.

Baseball is an allegorical play about America, a poetic, complex and subtle play of courage, fear, good luck, mistakes, patience about fate and sober self-esteem (batting average). It is impossible to understand America without a thorough knowledge of baseball.

Giacometti's Telephone

Giacometti lived for many years on a Parisian courtyard, a beautiful décor of French poverty. He installed a telephone, forced probably by his dealer. After each telephone call, as he was working very often directly in gesso and his hands were caked with plaster, the telephone became more a plaster sculpture by Giacometti, a sculpture that now and then would ring.

IN PARIS WITH PERRAULT'S CAT

The Tower of the Winds, in Athens

I went in search of the Tower of the Winds, the ancient octagonal temple dedicated to the eight winds that blow from the four cardinal points. During my first year as a student of architecture, I had built a complete reconstruction of this monument, using archaeological renderings and romantic photographs that looked as if they were made by the Turks, who had occupied the territory until the last century. This monument was extremely familiar to me. I knew it as if it were a friend or relative. I had it measured, and examined carefully all the engravings and photographs. I was walking hesitantly, for the emotion was similar to the one I could have had seeing a lover after twenty years. Finally, the tower appeared; it looked very small, like all things known when young and revisited years after. But so pleasant, so resembling itself, as if the lover of twenty years ago had preserved herself perfectly. Around it there was a great number of peddlers and a tailor shop with a marvelous sign representing an elegant Greek that could have been the envy of Magritte. Also goats, chickens, etc.

That winter in Russia was a trip for my nose, a voyage to the odors of Eastern Europe and my childhood — beautiful ones of winter and also of elementary school, police station, disinfectant, the terrible odor of fear which at that time, with Stalin only recently gone, permeated Moscow and Leningrad and even the countryside. Those ancient smells and emotions were like a visit to my past, a travel in time.

Nothing is lost of what the memory accumulates, an immense computer that continues to register and classify data that are used only in a minimal proportion for conventional and monotone life. Life in this sense is like a huge ocean liner in which only one cabin is used.

I stole the telephone directory of Samarkand — a great risk — the book was probably sacred state property. But irresistible. Mostly organizations, instructions for the proper use of the instrument; about a hundred subscribers, among them a Goldberg. 11-62 Гольдберг Д.П.

Traveled in Russia: Moscow, Leningrad, Odessa, Tbilisi, Tashkent and Samarkand.
Traveled in Alaska.

1956

Traveled in Spain.

Mural for the U.S. Pavilion at the Brussels World Fair.

Décor for *Count Ory,* a Rossini opera performed at the Juilliard.

Commissions of any sort — from the outside or self-inflicted — are in contradiction to the nature of the modern artist.

1957 *There are important years and obscure ones; '57 is an obscure one. What happened? In Spain we traveled in a never-seen-before Citroën DS19, a car that caused a sensation wherever we went. I was an object of curiosity. <u>They</u> learned something and I nothing.*
Now I drive a very common car, hard to recognize in a parking lot.

1958

In the beginning of the summer, I went by bus and rented car to Kentucky, Tennessee and West Virginia, visiting hillbilly places and people. These are the ancestors of the Americans, the heroes of our best fiction — cowboys, villains, country derelicts.
I ended properly, visiting Oxford, Mississippi. I still have the phone directory — many Faulkners and Falkners.

Bought house in Springs (East Hampton). 1959

The Labyrinth. Subjects explored: ILLUSION, TALKS, WOMEN, CATS, DOGS, BIRDS, THE CUBE, THE CROCODILE, THE MUSEUM, MOSCOW AND SAMARKAND (WINTER, 1956), OTHER EASTERN COUNTRIES, AMERICA, MOTELS, BASEBALL, HORSE RACING, BULLFIGHTS, ART, FROZEN MUSIC, WORDS, GEOMETRY, HEROES, HARPIES, ETC. 1960

With Sigrid in East Hampton

Life is seen here like a voyage from (birth) A to the end, B. Normal lives make simple, even geometric travels, tracks without surprises, lives determined by family, money, geography or even logical and normal disasters. There is another normality — that of the neurotic or insane, shown here only by the more disagreeable drawing.

The artist (and my idea of the artist, poet, painter, composer, etc., is the novelist) investigates all the other lives in order to understand the world and possibly himself before returning to his own, often for a short and dull time only. It accounts for the delayed (even retarded) nature of the artist.

Traveled in Kenya, Uganda and Ethiopia; Israel, India and Japan.

The New World, a book about: NUMBERS, CONCENTRIC CIRCLES, SPEECH, GEOMETRY, PARODIES OF PARODIES, DESCARTES, NEWTON, QUESTION MARKS, GIUSEPPE VERDI, DRAWING TABLES, THE DISASTERS OF FAME, MARKS AND ALLEGORIES.

Le Masque (texts by Michel Butor and Harold Rosenberg). Contents of *Le Masque:* SELF-DRAWN ARTISTS, ANACHRONISTIC LANDSCAPES, ART LOVERS, TREES, STILL LIVES OF ILLUSIONS, AIRMAIL VARIATIONS, LABEL COLLAGES, RECORDS, NAVAJOS, DUTCHMEN, SPHINXES AND HARPIES, COUPLES, THE NOSE, QUASI DAL VERO, PAPER-BAG MASKS AS COLLAGES OR PHOTOGRAPHED ON REAL PEOPLE BY INGE MORATH.

1964

1965

1966

East Africa stays as a vision of Paradise for the marvelous climate — the hot sun and cool air of the plateau with the incredible sight of the baobab, more impressive than any elephant. I spent several winters there until the sight of policemen with tommy guns made it clear that Uganda, like most of Africa, was out.

A pleasant memory is a trip to Murchison Falls with Saul Bellow in a small boat on the Nile, surrounded by hundreds of crocodiles — both of us terrified at the idea of disaster and comical obituaries.

For two days I wore a tag saying "NASA Artist." I had been invited to be inspired by the flight of Apollo, a scene that would have interested comic-strip artists, Delaunay or even Chagall and his flying Hasidim for the unexpectedly slow, solemn levitation of the missile. But I was much more interested in the honky-tonks around Cape Canaveral.

Inge Morath

244

Spent four months in Washington, D.C., as Artist-in-Residence at the Smithsonian Institution.

1967 *I spent four months in Washington in 1967. Perhaps the strangest four months of my life. I had the life of an immigrant in a country where normally there is no immigration — like Norway, for instance, or Albania. I lived in Georgetown in a house that looked like a Norwegian palace, fortunately belonging to a zoologist who specialized in gorillas — a perfect occasion to read as much as I wanted about them, including the fact that the elderly gorilla loses interest in social life, becomes a loner and follows the tribe from a certain distance. One of the most attractive things about the Smithsonian was its stationery. I made many drawings on it exploiting the excellent logo. In that period I also made four curtains for* L'Histoire du Soldat *of Stravinsky — performed, I think, in Seattle, Washington. And a scroll, thirty or forty feet long, a nice way of keeping a diary, ruined naturally by the boredom of a self-imposed commission.*

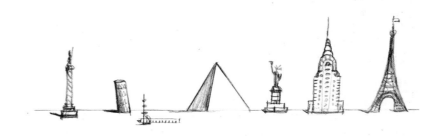

Traveled to Egypt: Cairo and Luxor.

The Inspector. PARADES, BIOGRAPHIES, MASKS, STREETS AND AVENUES, TIME AND SPACE, MUSIC-WRITING, RUBBER-STAMP ARCHITECTURE AND SOCIETY, THE PROFESSIONAL AVANT-GARDE, THE LAW OF GRAVITY, URBAN WAR, CLOUD FORMATIONS, WORDS AND LETTERS, CROCODILES, COWBOYS, GIRLS AND DINERS.

1973

Pyramids

The landscape has to be given scale by human presence. But the man alone makes it melancholy. Isolated monuments, like St. Peter's, the Eiffel Tower, or the Chrysler Building, would look like toys in a landscape. They are city stuff. Pyramids are perfect; nothing surpasses their beauty and intelligence as a solemn symbol of the human presence.

A retrospective.

1978

One-man exhibitions

1943	Wakefield Gallery, New York.
1945	Young Books, Inc., New York.
1948	Institute of Design, Chicago.
1950	Museum of Art, Rhode Island School of Design, Providence.
	Betty Parsons Gallery, New York.
1951	Galleria l'Obelisco, Rome.
1952	Galeria de Arte, São Paulo.
	Museu de Arte, São Paulo.
	Gump's Gallery, San Francisco.
	Institute of Contemporary Arts, London.
	Sidney Janis Gallery, New York.
	Kunsthalle, Wuppertal-Barmen, West Germany.
	Leopold-Hoesch-Museum, Düren, West Germany.
	Galleria l'Obelisco, Rome.
	Betty Parsons Gallery, New York.
	Frank Perls Gallery, Beverly Hills, California.
1953	Arts Club of Chicago.
	Galerie Blanche, Stockholm.
	Galerie Maeght, Paris.
	Stedelijk Museum, Amsterdam.
	Virginia Museum of Fine Arts, Richmond.
1954	Corcoran Gallery of Art, Washington, D.C.
	Dallas Museum of Fine Arts.
	Museum am Ostwall, Dortmund, West Germany.
	Frankfurter Kunstkabinett, Frankfurt.
	Kestner-Gesellschaft, Hannover.
	Kunstmuseum, Basel.
	Santa Barbara Museum, Santa Barbara, California.
1955	Harvard School of Design, Cambridge, Massachusetts.
1956	Allan Frumkin Gallery, Chicago.
1957	Institute of Contemporary Arts, London.
1959	Musée d'Art Moderne, Brussels.
1962	The Art Gallery, University of California, Santa Barbara.
1965	Davison Art Center, Wesleyan University, Middletown, Connecticut.
1966	Sidney Janis Gallery, New York.
	Galerie Maeght, Paris.
	Betty Parsons Gallery, New York.
	Wallraf-Richartz-Museum, Cologne.
1967	B. C. Holland Gallery, Chicago.
	Musée d'Art Moderne, Brussels.
	Museum Boymans-van Beuningen, Rotterdam.
	Obelisk Gallery, Boston.
	Musées Royaux des Beaux-Arts de Belgique, Brussels.
1968	Museo de Bellas Artes, Caracas.
	Hamburger Kunsthalle, Hamburg.
	Irving Galleries, Milwaukee.
	Louisiana Museum, Humlebaek, Denmark.
	Moderna Museet, Stockholm.
1969	J.L. Hudson Gallery, Detroit.
	Sidney Janis Gallery, New York.
	Betty Parsons Gallery, New York.
1970	Felix Landau Gallery, Los Angeles.
1971	Richard Gray Gallery, Chicago.
	Galerie Maeght, Paris and Zurich.
1973	Galleria Galatea, Milan.
	Sidney Janis Gallery, New York.
	Galerie Maeght, Paris.
	Betty Parsons Gallery, New York.
1973–1974	National Collection of Fine Arts, Smithsonian Institution, Washington, D.C.
1974	Institute of Contemporary Arts, Boston.
	Galerie Maeght, Paris.
1974–1975	Traveling exhibition organized by Kölnischer Kunstverein, Cologne (Württembergischer Kunstverein, Stuttgart; Kestner-Gesellschaft, Hannover; Kulturhaus der Stadt Graz; Museum des 20. Jahrhunderts, Vienna).
1976	Sidney Janis Gallery, New York.
	Betty Parsons Gallery, New York.
1977	Galerie Maeght, Paris and Zurich.

Selected group exhibitions

1946	Museum of Modern Art, New York. *Fourteen Americans*.
1949	Detroit Institute of Arts. *An Exhibition for Modern Living*.
	Museum of Modern Art, New York. *Art Directors' Club: 28th Annual Exhibition of Advertising and Editorial Art of the New York Art Directors' Club*.
	Whitney Museum of American Art, New York. *Annual Exhibition of Contemporary American Sculpture, Watercolors, and Drawings*.
1952	Art Institute of Chicago. *Contemporary Drawings from 12 Countries: 1945–1952*.
	Walker Art Center, Minneapolis. *Contemporary American Painting and Sculpture. Collection of Mr. and Mrs. Roy R. Neuberger*.
1953	American Federation of Arts, New York. *American Caricatures* (traveling exhibition).
	Brandeis University, Waltham, Massachusetts. *The Comic Spirit*.
1954	Milan. *X Triennale in Milano*.
	Whitney Museum of American Art, New York. *The Roy and Marie Neuberger Collection* (traveling exhibition).
1957	Brooklyn Museum, New York. *Golden Years of American Drawings: 1905–1956*.
1958	Fort Worth Art Center, Fort Worth, Texas. *The Iron Horse in Art: The Railroad as It Has Been Interpreted by Artists of the 19th and 20th Centuries*.
	Frederiksberg Town Hall, Copenhagen. *World Cartoonists*.
	United States Pavilion, World's Fair, Brussels. *Expo '58*.
1962	Horace Mann School, Riverdale, New York. *Modern American Art Selected from the Collection of Mr. and Mrs. Harris B. Steinberg*.
	Norfolk Museum of Arts and Sciences, Norfolk, Virginia. *American Drawing Annual XIX*.
1964	UNESCO. *Die Kunst der Schrift* (traveling exhibition).
1965	Whitney Museum of American Art, New York. *A Decade of American Drawings: 1955–1965*.
	New School Art Center, New York. *Portraits from the American Art World*.
1966	The Art Gallery, University of California, Santa Barbara. *A Selection of Paintings, Drawings, Collages, and Sculpture from the Collection of Mr. and Mrs. Billy Wilder*.
	Kunstverein und Akademie der Künste, Berlin. *Labyrinthe*.
	Musée d'Art Moderne, Palais de Tokyo, Paris. *23rd Salon de Mai*.
1967	Kunsthalle, Darmstadt, West Germany. *Zweite International der Zeichnung*.
1968	Finch College Museum of Art, New York. *Documentation: Sculpture—Painting—Drawing*.
	Kunstverein, Frankfurt. *Aus dem Traumbuch der Maler*.
	Museum of Art, Rhode Island School of Design, Providence. *An American Collection. The Neuberger Collection: Paintings, Drawings and Sculpture*.
1969	Fort Worth Art Center Museum, Fort Worth, Texas. *Drawings*.
1969–1970	New School Art Center, New York. *American Drawings of the Sixties: A Selection*.
1970	American Federation of Arts, New York. *The Drawing Society National Exhibition: 1970* (traveling exhibition).
	Museum of Art, Carnegie Institute, Pittsburgh, Pennsylvania. *Carnegie International Exhibition of Painting and Sculpture*.
	Fondation Maeght, St.-Paul-de-Vence, France. *L'Art vivant aux États-Unis*.
	Sidney Janis Gallery, New York. *Seven Artists*.
	Sidney Janis Gallery, New York. *String and Rope*.
1971	Art Institute of Chicago. *31st Annual Exhibition: Works on Paper*.
	Bibliothèque Nationale, Paris. *Le Dessin d'humour*.
	Corcoran Gallery of Art, Washington, D.C. *Seven Enormously Popular American Artists*.
1972	Kunsthalle, Recklinghausen, West Germany. *Zeitgenossen karikieren Zeitgenossen*.
	Kunsthaus, Zurich. *Karikatur-Karikatur*.
1973	Yale University Art Gallery, New Haven, Connecticut. *American Drawing 1970–1973*.
1974	Galerie Beyeler, Basel. *Surréalismus et peinture*.
	Cleveland Museum of Art. *Contemporary American Artists*.
1974–1975	Cleveland Museum of Art. *American Artists*.
1974	Downtown Branch of the Whitney Museum of American Art, New York. *25 Stills*.
1975–1976	Sidney Janis Gallery, New York. *Realism and Reality*.
1976	Akron Art Institute, Akron, Ohio. *Contemporary Images in Watercolor*.
1977	Hamilton Gallery of Contemporary Art, New York. *Drawing Today in New York*.
	Documenta Druck Verlag GmbH, Kassel, West Germany. *Documenta 6*.
	Minnesota Museum of Art, St. Paul. *American Drawing: 1927–1977*.
	Renwick Gallery, Smithsonian Institution, Washington, D.C. *The Object as Poet*.

Selected exhibition catalogues

Fourteen Americans. Edited by Dorothy C. Miller. New York: Museum of Modern Art, 1946.

An Exhibition for Modern Living. Edited by A. H. Girard and W. D. Laurie, Jr. Detroit: Detroit Institute of Arts, 1949.

Steinberg. Rome: Galleria l'Obelisco, 1951.

Contemporary American Painting and Sculpture. Collection of Mr. and Mrs. Roy R. Neuberger. Minneapolis: Walker Art Center, 1952.

Saul Steinberg. London: Institute of Contemporary Arts, 1952.

Steinberg Drawings. Beverly Hills, California: Frank Perls Gallery, 1952.

Saul Steinberg. Amsterdam: Stedelijk Museum, 1953.

Saul Steinberg. Derrière le Miroir no. 53/54. Paris: Galerie Maeght, 1953.

Steinberg. Stockholm: Galerie Blanche, 1953.

Steinberg Drawings. Chicago: Arts Club of Chicago, 1953.

The Roy and Marie Neuberger Collection. New York: Whitney Museum of American Art, 1954.

Saul Steinberg. Dortmund, West Germany: Museum am Ostwall, 1954.

Steinberg. Text by Alfred Hentzen. Hannover: Kestner-Gesellschaft, 1954.

The Iron Horse in Art: The Railroad as It Has Been Interpreted by Artists of the 19th and 20th Centuries. Foreword by Lucius Beebe. Fort Worth, Texas: Fort Worth Art Center, 1958.

Steinberg. Derrière le Miroir no. 157. Paris: Galerie Maeght, 1966.

Steinberg Aquarelles, Dessins et Collages: 1955–1967. Introduction by Pierre Baudson. Brussels: Musées Royaux des Beaux-Arts de Belgique, 1967.

Steinberg. Text by Pierre Baudson. Rotterdam: Museum Boymans-van Beuningen, 1967.

An American Collection. The Neuberger Collection: Paintings, Drawings and Sculpture. Foreword by Daniel Robbins and David W. Scott; preface by Roy R. Neuberger; introduction by Daniel Robbins. Providence: Museum of Art, Rhode Island School of Design, 1968.

Documentation: Sculpture—Painting—Drawing. Text by Elayne H. Varian. New York: Finch College Museum of Art, 1968.

Exposición Saul Steinberg. Caracas: Museo de Bellas Artes, 1968.

Saul Steinberg. Humlebaek, Denmark: Louisiana Museum, 1968.

Saul Steinberg. Teckningar och collage: 1955–67. Stockholm: Moderna Museet, 1968.

Steinberg: Zeichnungen und Collagen. Foreword by Helmut Leppien; essays by Pierre Baudson and Manuel Gasser; interview by André Parinaud. Hamburg: Hamburger Kunsthalle, 1968.

L'Art vivant aux États-Unis. St.-Paul-de-Vence, France: Fondation Maeght, 1970.

Paintings and Drawings/Saul Steinberg. Los Angeles: Felix Landau Gallery, 1970.

Le Dessin d'humour. Paris: Bibliothèque National, 1971.

Steinberg 1971. Essay by Jacques Dupin. *Derrière le Miroir* no. 192. Paris: Galerie Maeght, 1971.

Steinberg: Ölbilder, Gouachen, Zeichnungen. Text by Manuel Gasser. Zurich: Galerie Maeght, 1971.

New Work by Saul Steinberg. New York: Sidney Janis Gallery, 1973.

Steinberg. "Tables d'Évidences," by Hubert Damisch. *Derrière le Miroir* no. 205. Paris: Galerie Maeght, 1973.

Steinberg at the Smithsonian. Foreword by John Hollander. Washington, D.C.: National Collection of Fine Arts, Smithsonian Institution Press, 1973.

Saul Steinberg: Zeichnungen, Aquarelle, Collagen, Gemälde, Reliefs (1963–74). Cologne: Kölnischer Kunstverein, 1974.

American Drawing: 1927–1977. Prologue by Miriam B. Lein; essay by Paul Cummings; catalogue notes by Sandra L. Lipshultz. St. Paul: Minnesota Museum of Art, 1977.

Documenta 6. Kassel, West Germany: Paul Dierichs KG & Co., 1977.

The Object as Poet. Washington, D.C.: Smithsonian Institution Press, 1977.

Steinberg. "La Plume à la première personne," by Italo Calvino. *Derrière le Miroir* no. 224. Paris: Galerie Maeght, 1977.

Books by Saul Steinberg

All in Line. New York: Duell, Sloan & Pearce, 1945.

The Art of Living. New York: Harper & Bros., 1949.

The Passport. New York: Harper & Bros., 1954.

Steinberg's Umgang mit Menschen. Hamburg: Rowohlt Verlag, 1954.

Dessins. Paris: Gallimard, 1956.

The Labyrinth. New York: Harper & Row, 1960.

The Catalogue. Cleveland: Meridian Books/World Publishing Co., 1962.

Steinberg's Paperback. Hamburg: Rowohlt Taschenbuch Verlag GmbH, 1964.

The New World. New York: Harper & Row, 1965.

Le Masque. Texts by Michel Butor and Harold Rosenberg; photographs by Inge Morath. Paris: Maeght Editeur, 1966.

The Inspector. New York: Viking Press, 1973.

Selected bibliography

Adhémar, Jean. *20th Century Graphics*. New York: Praeger Publishers, 1971.

Bauer, John I. H. *Revolution and Tradition in Modern American Art*. Cambridge, Mass.: Harvard University Press, 1958.

Biddle, George. *The Yes and No of Contemporary Art: An Artist's Evaluation*. Cambridge, Mass.: Harvard University Press, 1957.

Chaet, Bernard. *The Art of Drawing*. New York: Holt, Rinehart & Winston, 1970 (?).

China Theater. An Informal Notebook of Useful Information for Military Men in China. Illustrations by Saul Steinberg. Office of Strategic Services, c. 1943–1945.

Claus, Jürgen. *Kunst heute*. Hamburg: Rowohlt Taschenbuch Verlag GmbH, 1965.

Cummings, Paul. *American Drawings: The 20th Century*. New York: Studio Book/Viking Press, 1976.

——— . *Dictionary of Contemporary American Artists*. 3rd ed. New York: St. Martin's Press, 1977.

Gill, Brendan. *Here at The New Yorker*. New York: Random House, 1975.

Gombrich, E. H. *Art and Illusion*. Bollingen Series XXV/5. New York: Pantheon Books, 1960.

Green, Samuel M. *American Art: A Historical Survey*. New York: Ronald Press, 1966.

Gruen, John. *The Party's Over Now*. New York: Viking Press, 1972.

Hayes, Bartlett H., Jr. *American Drawings. Drawings of the Masters*. New York: Shorewood Publishers, 1965.

Hofmann, Werner. *Caricature from Leonardo to Picasso*. New York: Crown Publishers, 1957.

Kramer, Hilton. *The Age of the Avant-Garde. An Art Chronicle of 1965–1972*. New York: Farrar, Straus & Giroux, 1973.

Kris, E., and Gombrich, E. H. *Caricature*. Middlesex, England: King Penguin Books, 1940.

METRO: International Directory of Contemporary Art. Milan: Metro, 1964.

Nemerov, Howard. *The Next Room of the Dream*. Chicago: University of Chicago Press, 1962.

The New Yorker Album of Drawings: 1925–1975. New York: Viking Press, 1975.

Rodman, Selden. *The Insiders*. Baton Rouge: Louisiana State University Press, 1960.

——— . *Conversations with Artists*. Introduction by Alexander Eliot. New York: Capricorn Books, 1961.

Rosenberg, Harold. *The Anxious Object*. New York: Horizon Press, 1964.

——— . *Artworks and Packages*. New York: Horizon Press, 1969.

——— . *The De-definition of Art. Action Art to Pop to Earthworks*. New York: Horizon Press, 1972.

——— . *Discovering the Present: Three Decades in Art, Culture, and Politics*. Chicago: University of Chicago Press, 1972.

Sachs, Paul J. *Modern Prints & Drawings*. Preface by Alfred H.

Barr, Jr. New York: Alfred A. Knopf, 1954.

Schneider, Pierre. *Louvre Dialogues.* New York: Atheneum, 1971.

Seitz, William. *The Art of Assemblage.* New York: Museum of Modern Art, 1961.

Stebbins, Theodore E., Jr. *American Master Drawings and Watercolors.* New York: Harper & Row, 1976.

Tillich, Paul. *My Search for Absolutes.* New York: Simon & Schuster, 1967.

Trier, Eduard. *Zeichner des XX. Jahrhunderts.* Berlin: Mann, 1956.

Wilson, Edmund. *Letters on Literature and Politics: 1912–1972.* Edited by Elena Wilson; introduction by Daniel Aaron; foreword by Leon Edel. New York: Farrar, Straus & Giroux, 1977.

Witttkamp, Franz. *Saul Steinberg oder Philosophie der Zeichnung.* Mainz: Gesellschaft für bildende Kunst, 1971.

Periodicals

"After Hours." *Harper's* (June 1948).

"L'Air de Paris. Steinberg a dessiné à Milan un labyrinthe pour aveugles." *Arts* (Paris) (September 15–21, 1954).

"American Academy of Arts and Letters Awards Cartoonist Saul Steinberg Its Medal for Graphic Arts." *New York Times* (May 23, 1974).

"Art" [review of *Art of Living*]. *Time* (September 26, 1949).

"Art: Hard Lines." *Time* (October 18, 1954).

Ashbery, John. "Saul Steinberg: The Stamp of Genius." *Art News* 68 (November 1969).

———. "Saul Steinberg: Callibiography." *Art News Annual* 36 (1970).

Ashton, Dore. "The Symbol Lurking in the Wings." *Studio International* 173 (February 1967).

"As Steinberg Sees It." *Newsweek* (June 6, 1955).

[Astragal]. "Notes and Topics: Drawing the Crowds" [review of ICA exhibition]. *Architect's Journal* (May 8, 1952).

Aubusson, Brice. "Un Dessinateur, témoin de l'époque." *Le Courrier de la Presse Le Matin* (April 21, 1951).

[E. B.] "Steinberg ou la pêche à la ligne." *Les Beaux-Arts* 809 (April 18, 1958).

Barry, Iris. "Seeing Through Things" [review of *All in Line*]. *New York Herald Tribune Weekly Book Review* (June 17, 1945).

———. "Uncanny Comic Innocence" [review of *Art of Living*]. *New York Herald Tribune* (November 6, 1949).

Beauvais, Patricia. "Steinberg ne dessine plus qu'avec des tampons." *Paris Match* (June 1971).

Bedient, Calvin. "S for Steinberg." *Partisan Review* 41, no. 4 (1974).

Bell, Jane. "Reviews." *New York Arts* 47 (April 1973).

Benedikt, M. "New York Letter." *Art International* 11, no. 1 (January 20, 1967).

Bernstein, Walter. [Review of *All in Line*]. *New York Times* (July 15, 1945).

Billetdoux, François. "Steinberg." *Arts* (Paris) 410 (May 8, 1953).

"Bizarre Little Creations of Steinberg." *Life* (August 13, 1945).

Boice, Bruce. "Reviews." *Artforum* 11 (May 1973).

Bone, Stephen. "Saul Steinberg's Drawings" [review of ICA exhibition]. *Manchester Guardian* (May 2, 1952).

Boswell, P. "Peyton Boswell Comments" [editorial]. *Art Digest* (September 15, 1946).

Bouret, Jean. "Les Papiers du Barnabooth's Club" [review of Galerie Maeght exhibition]. *Nouvelles Littéraires* (May 26, 1977).

Buresch, Roman. "Warten auf Steinberg." *Die Zeit* 13 (August 4, 1967).

Bürger, W. "Sights and Sounds." *New Masses* (October 8, 1946).

Buzzi, Aldo. "L'Architetto Steinberg." *Domus* 214 (October 1946).

[R. C.] "Cinq Minutes avec Steinberg qui, pour compléter sa collection, a acheté à Paris un chapeau de gendarme." *Carrefour* (April 29, 1953).

C[ampbell], L[awrence]. "Reviews and Previews." *Art News* 65 (December 1966).

Canaday, John. "46 L.I. Artists Brush Up for Politics." *New York Times* (August 19, 1972).

———: [Review of *The Inspector*]. *New York Times Book Review* (April 1, 1973).

"Les Caricaturistes dénoncent les vicissitudes du monde moderne." *Du* (Zurich) (May 28–June 3, 1958).

Caso, Paul. "Les Dessins de Steinberg au Musée d'Art Moderne." *Le Soir* (Brussels) (March 16, 1967).

Castans, Raymond. "Steinberg, premier dessinateur américain." *Paris Match* (April 14, 1951).

Cator, B. "Saul Steinberg" [review of traveling exhibition]. *Kunstwerk* (Stuttgart) (January 6, 1975).

Chapsal, Madeleine. "Steinberg." *La Quinzaine Littéraire* 3 (April 15, 1966).

Chéry, Christian. "Saul Steinberg." *Les Lettres Françaises* (April 6, 1966).

"Chez Atmosphere." *Harper's* (November 1949).

Choay, Françoise. "L'Art vivant à l'Expo de Bruxelles." *L'Oeil* 42 (June 1958).

Cianetti, Franco. "Portrait." *Camera* (March 1967).

Clair, Jean. "Steinberg à Paris." *L'Art Vivant* 21 (June 1971).

Clasen, Wolfgang. "'Cartoons' aus dem Amerika von Heute." *Kunstwerk* 7, no. 5 (1953).

Constable, Rosalind. "Saul Steinberg, a Profile." *Art Digest* (February 1, 1954).

Curjel, Hans. "Expo '58." *Graphis* 14 (1958).

"Curtain Goes Up." *New York World-Telegram* (September 14, 1946).

da Silva, Quirino. "Steinberg." *Diário de São Paulo* (September 21, 1952).

———. "Considerações à margem." *Diário de São Paulo* (September 28, 1952).

Daval, Jean-Luc. "Chagall et Steinberg, deux narrateurs." *Art International* 15 (October 20, 1971).

Davenport, Basil. [Review of *Art of Living*]. *Book-of-the-Month Club News* (New York) (December 1949).

Degand, Léon. "Steinberg—dessinateur et humoriste." *Le Soir* (Brussels) (May 19, 1953).

"Department of the Rubber Stamp" [editorial]. *Harper's Bazaar* (June 1959).

de Rivoyre, Christine. "Avec Steinberg poète, architecte, et faussaire." *Le Monde* (Paris) (April 24, 1953).

Devree, Howard. "It's Funny—But Is It Art?" *New York Times Magazine* (September 8, 1946).

"Drawings at the I.C.A. Gallery." *Apollo* (June 1952).

Dukeminier, Jesse, Jr. "Lynn: The Modern Rule Against Perpetuities." *Yale Law Journal* 77, no. 1 (November 1967).

Dupin, Jacques. "Steinberg et le Société anonyme." *XXᵉ Siècle* (Paris) n. s. 40 (June 1973).

Eichholz, Armin. "Affenliebe zur Malerei. Possen mit tierischem Ernst." *Kunst* 60 (1961–1962).

"8 Medal Awards Made in Ad and Editorial Art." *New York Herald Tribune* (June 2, 1948).

Einhaus, Lambert. "Partituren der Gebärde." *Frankfurter Allgemeine Zeitung* (January 26, 1954).

Elgar, Frank. "Steinberg révélé aux hommes ce qu'ils connaissent le moins: eux-mêmes." *Carrefour* (April 29, 1953).

Emmerich, André. "The Artist as Collector." *Art in America* 46, no. 2 (Summer 1958).

Eres, George. "In Search of Nudes." *Independent* (Long Beach, Calif.) (July 1, 1951).

Erler, Martin. "Saul Steinberg deutsche Premiere: Mit Ipitzer Feder." *Bremer Nachrichten* (January 15, 1954).

"Exhibitions at the Sidney Janis and Betty Parsons Galleries." *Interiors* 111 (March 1952).

Fabian, Rainer. "Cartoons von Saul Steinberg—Linien eines Philosophen." *Die Welt* 184 (August 9, 1973).

"False Daguerreotypes, and False Diary; False Diploma, True Steinberg." *Vogue* (October 15, 1954).

Farber, Manny: "An American Show." *New Republic* (October 14, 1946).

Fischer, Wend. "Saul Steinberg graphische Kabarett." *Neue Ruhr-Zeitung* (Essen) (January 25, 1957).

Fitzsimmons, James. "Strolling Kibitzer" [exhibition review]. *Art Digest* (February 1, 1952).

"For Eloquence and Precision." *Publishers Weekly* 183 (June 3, 1963).

Forssell, Lars. "Anteckning till Steinberg." *Konstrevy* (Stockholm) 1 (1954).

"14 Members Are Chosen by National Arts Institute." *New York Times* (March 5, 1968).

Frankenstein, Alfred. "A Critical View of the Exhibits at the City's Art Galleries." *San Francisco Chronicle* (May 18, 1947).

———. "This World: A Tour Through the Art Galleries." *San Francisco Chronicle* (March 16, 1952).

Fremont-Smith, Eliot. "Books of the Times: Santa's Helpers, Cartoonists All" [review of *The New World*]. *New York Times* (December 6, 1965).

Fussell, B. H. "Show Steinberg Satiric, Amusing at Lyman Allyn." *Day* (New London, Conn.) (November 13, 1953).

[J. G.] "Story of Life Keeps in Line." *New Zealand Herald* (July 15, 1961).

Gablik, Suzi. "Meta-trompe-l'oeil." *Art News* 64 (March 1965).

Gallego, J. "Steinberg y la administración." *Goya* 104 (September 1971).

Gannett, Lewis. "Books and Things" [review of *Art of Living*]. *New York Herald Tribune* (December 6, 1949).

Gasser, Manuel. "Verner Witting." *Graphis* 49 (1953).

———. "Steinberg sur des nouvelles pistes." *Graphis* 10, no. 53 (1954).

———. "Steinberg as an Advertising Artist." *Graphis* 12 (September 1956).

———. "Gezeichnete Ironie." *Graphis* 15 (November 1959).

———. "Saul Steinberg." *Graphis* 21, no. 117 (1965).

———. "Saul Steinberg: Le Masque." *Graphis* 22, no. 123 (1966).

———. "Saul Steinberg" [photographs by Franco Cianetti]. *Du-Atlantis* (August 26, 1966).

Gaudet, Michel. "La Peinture: Steinberg à la Fondation Maeght." *Le Patriote* (October 30, 1966).

"La Gazette d'Adrienne Monnier. Les Dessins de Steinberg." *Les Lettres Nouvelles* (Paris) 7 (September 1953).

G[ebhard], D[avid]. "Saul Steinberg and Paul Klee." *Artforum* 1 (February 1963).

"G.I. Sketchbook." *Time* (June 18, 1945).

Gilroy, Harry. "Institute of Arts Presents Awards." *New York Times* (May 29, 1968).

Glavimans, A. "Niets ontgaat Saul Steinberg." *Algemeen Dagblad* (May 2, 1953).

Glozer, Lazlo. "Der Inspektor von Saul Steinberg." *Süddeutsche Zeitung* 172 (July 28–29, 1973).

Glueck, Grace. [Review of *The Labyrinth*]. *New York Times Book Review* (January 15, 1961).

———. "New York Gallery Notes." *Art in America* 57 (November 1969).

———. "A Way to Stamp Out Art." *New York Times* (November 9, 1969).

———. "The Artist Speaks: Saul Steinberg." *Art in America* 58 (November–December 1970).

Gosling, Nigel. "Steinberg" [review of ICA exhibition]. *The Observer* (London) (May 11, 1952).

Gottlieb, Gerald. [Review of *The Passport*]. *New York Herald Tribune Book Review* (December 5, 1954).

Gould, Ray. "Steinberg's Satirical Art in Book; Absurdities Superb 'Example of Irony'" [review of *All in Line*]. *Advertiser* (Montgomery, Ala.) (July 22, 1945).

Greene, Balcomb. "14 Americans." *NYC: MKR's Art Outlook* (October 7, 1946).

Guéguen, Pierre. "L'Exposition Steinberg chez Maeght." *Art d'Aujourd'hui* 4, no. 6 (August 1953).

Hakanson, Joy. "Steinberg Aims Pen as Modern Living." *News* (Detroit) (August 28, 1949).

Halstead, Whitney. "Chicago" [review of Holland Gallery exhibition]. *Artform* 5 (April 1967).

Mr. Harper [Russell Lynes]. "Steinberg's Stuff." *Harper's* (April 1952).

Henry, Gerrit. "Reviews and Previews." *Art News* 72 (April 1973).

Hess, Thomas B. "Saul Steinberg vs. the Mickey Mouse Mugger." *New York* (March 5, 1973).

———. "Drawing 'Einstein on the Beach.'" *New York* (December 13, 1976).

Hicks, Granville. "Connoisseur of the Incongruous" [review of *The Labyrinth*]. *Saturday Review of Literature* (January 7, 1961).

Hickson, Elizabeth. "The Navy Locked Away Mr. S's 'Secret' Plans" [review of ICA exhibition]. *Daily Mirror* (London) (May 2, 1952).

Hølaas, Af Odd. "Paa udkik efter den interssante grimhed." *Politiken* (December 14, 1958).

Hollander, John. [Review of *The Inspector*]. *Commentary* 56 (July 1973).

———. [Review of *The Inspector*]. *Choice* (Middletown, Conn.) 10 (November 1973).

Holstein, Bent. "Parafraser over livet." *Fyens Stiftstidende* (March 8, 1968).

Horton, Philip. "Steinberg's Ferocious Sunglasses." *Reporter* (December 1954).

"*The Inspector*, by S. Steinberg" [review]. *Commentary* 56 (July 1973).

Ionesco, Eugène. "La Tragédie du langage." *Spectacles* (July 1958).

———. "Steinberg: Artistes." *Connaissance des Arts* 303 (May 1977).

Jackson, Joseph Henry. "Bookman's Notebook" [review of *All in Line*]. *San Francisco Chronicle* (June 21, 1945).

"J'Enseigne aux hommes à nager en les poussant dans l'eau" [interview with André Parinaud]. *Arts et Loisirs* 25 (March 16–22, 1966).

"Job of Being Absurd." *Newsweek* (July 9, 1945).

Joss of 'The Star.' "Steinberg." *Art News and Review* (London) (May 17, 1952).

Jouffroy, Alain. "Steinberg i Paris." *Palatten* (Göteborg, Sweden) 2 (1955).

———. "Un Grand Dessinateur américain, Saul Steinberg, juge la peinture abstraite, le Salon des Indépendants et Picasso." *Arts* (Paris) (May 11–17, 1955).

———. "Psychoanalyse de Saul Steinberg." *Arts* (Paris) (May 28–June 3, 1958).

———. "De la rapidité de Steinberg à la lenteur de Baj." *Metro* (Milan) 3 (1961).

———. "Visite à Saul Steinberg." *Opus International* (Paris) 29, no. 30 (December 1971).

———. "Le Grand Jeu de Lindner." *XXᵉ Siècle* (Paris) 42 (June 1974).

Jouffroy, Jean-Pierre. "Le Roi Saul." *Humanité Dimanche* 67 (May 11–17, 1977).

Karrer-Kharberg, Rolf. "Steinberg." *Die Zeit*, 34 (August 23, 1963).

———. "Umgang mit Menschen." *Die Zeit*, 10 (March 7, 1969).

Keller, Heinz. "Saul Steinberg und die Architektur." *Werk* 44, no. 2 (1957).

Kozloff, M[ax]. "Art." *Nation* 203 (December 19, 1966).

Kramer, Hilton. "The Comic Fantasies of Saul Steinberg." *New York Times* (December 4, 1966).

———. "Steinberg: Latest Works." *New York Times* (November 8, 1969).

———. "Saul Steinberg: Vision, Satire, and Delight." *New York Times* (November 9, 1969).

———. "Steinberg's Surprises Mark Two Shows" [review]. *New York Times* (February 17, 1973).

Lascaut, Gilbert. "Aventures d'une horizontale." *L'Art Vivant* 21 (June 1971).

———. "Les Tableaux Tables de Steinberg" [exhibition review]. *L'Art Vivant* 43 (October 18, 1973).

———. "Steinberg et son monde de la métamorphose" [review of Galerie Maeght exhibition]. *La Quinzaine Littéraire* (May 16–31, 1977).

Legrand, Francine-Claire. "Expo 58. Regards sur l'art moderne." *Quadrum* 5 (1958).

Lepetit, P. "L'Inspecteur Steinberg" [book review]. *L'Architecture d'Aujourd'hui* 172 (March 1974).

[Letter to the Editor]. *New York Times* (November 27, 1966).

Litvinoff, Emanuel. "Conversation with Steinberg." *Jewish Observer & Middle East Review* 1 (May 30, 1952).

L[ouchheim], A[line] B. "Steinberg: Line of Fancy." *Art News* 44 (July 1945).

———. "Favored Few: Exhibition, Museum of Modern Art." *Art News* 45 (September 1946).

———. "Steinberg: Artist and Humorist." *New York Times* (February 3, 1952).

Lubell, Ellen. "Reviews." *New York Arts* 47 (April 1973).

Lukacs, John A. "Passport Review." *Commonweal* (December 3, 1954).

Lynes, Russell. "Man Named Steinberg." *Harper's* 209 (August 1954).

———. "Steinberg and the Others." *Harper's* 231 (December 1965).

[N. M.] "Cartoons von Saul Steinberg." *Werk* 41 (April 1954).

McCallum, Ian. "Labyrinth at Milan." *Art Review* 116 (December 1954).

"The Mad World of Cartoonists" [review of *All in Line*]. *New York Times* (July 15, 1945).

"Man Over Crocodile." *Newsweek* (December 26, 1960).

"Man in a Paper Mask." *Sunday Times* (London) (March 29, 1959).

Marc, André. "Exposition des 'Oeuvres murales' qui décoraient le pavillon U.S. de l'Expo 58 et des dessins du caricaturiste américain Steinberg au Palais des Beaux-Arts de Bruxelles." *La Lanterne* (Brussels) (March 28, 1967).

Marijnissen, R. H. "Saul Steinberg uit de Kelders naar de wand." *De Standaard* (Brussels) (March 22, 1967).

Martine, Claude. "Steinberg délivre un passeport pour les USA." *Arts* (Paris) 492 (December 1–7, 1954).

Masuda, Y. "L'Art de Saul Steinberg." *Mizue* (Tokyo) 578 (October 1953).

Mayne, Richard. "Passport Review." *New Statesman and Nation* (December 4, 1954).

Melville, Robert. [Review of *The Inspector*]. *New Statesman and Nation* (June 22, 1973).

"Message in the Medium." *Time* (April 15, 1966).

Metken, G. "Das Gesetz der Serie; wie Künstler comic nutzen." *Kunstwerk* 24 (September 1971).

Meyer, Karl E. "Steinberg Looks at Washington." *Washington Post* (March 15, 1970).

Michel, Jacques. "Lorsque l'humoriste se fait peintre—Les Parodies de Steinberg." *Le Monde* (June 24–30, 1971).

———. "Une 'Introspective' de Saul Steinberg" [interview]. *Le Monde* (June 5–6, 1977).

Middleton, M. H. "Art Exhibitions." *The Spectator* (London) (May 9, 1952).

Moholy-Nagy, Sibyl. "Images of Our Dilemma" [review of *The Passport*]. *Progressive Architecture* 36 (March 1955).

"Movie News: An Artist for Kelly." *New York Herald Tribune* (June 30, 1950).

Mueller, L. "Steinberg and High School Composition." *English Journal* 60 (November 1971).

"Mural in Milan." *L'Oeil* (Paris) 23 (1964).

"Murals by Modern Masters: Hotel Decoration." *Design* 54 (November 1952).

Naef, Hans. "Steinberg, Humorous Artist." *Graphis* 5, no. 26 (1949).

Neuman, Vivian, and Burnet, Mary. "Mostly About People." *New York Herald Tribune* (Paris) (March 7, 1951).

"New Show at the Modern" [review]. *New York Times* (September 22, 1946).

"News from Nowheresville." *Architectural Review* 130 (December 1961).

Newton, Eric. "Round the London Art Galleries" [review of ICA exhibition]. *The Listener* (May 15, 1952).

Nikolajsen, Ejgil. "Livets Krummelvrer." *Berlingske Tidendes Kronik* (March 2, 1968).

"Notes on Exhibition at Wakefield." *New York Herald Tribune* (April 18, 1943).

O'Connor, John J. "Art for Sale." *Wall Street Journal* (December 20, 1966).

[Pamplemousse]. "Les Caricatures monumentales de Steinberg." *Pan* (Brussels) (March 29, 1967).

Pendennis. "Table Talk" [review of ICA exhibition]. *The Observer* (London) (May 4, 1952).

———. "Table Talk." *The Observer* (London) (October 19, 1958).

Peppiatt, Michael. "Paris." *Art News* 73 (January 1974).

———. [Review of Galerie Maeght exhibition]. *Art International* (Paris) 18 (January 1974).

Pitz, H. C. "Saul Steinberg: Mad, Savage, Enigma?" *American Artist* 15 (February 1951).

Plagens, Peter. "Felix Landau Gallery, Los Angeles" [review]. *Artforum* 9 (February 1971).

Plant, A. S. [Review of *The Labryinth*]. *Library Journal* (December 1, 1954).

Politzer, Heinz. "The World of Saul Steinberg: A Mirror Reflecting the Forlornness of Modern Man." *Commentary* 4, no. 4 (October 1947).

Poore, Charles. "Books of the Times" [review of *Art of Living*]. *New York Times* (October 8, 1949).

———. "Books of the Times: Ancient and Modern Art" [review of *The Passport*]. *New York Times* (October 7, 1954).

P[orter], F[airfield]. "Reviews and Previews." *Art News* 50 (February 1952).

Propes, A. W. [Review of *The Inspector*]. *Commentary* 56 (July 1973).

———. [Review of *The Inspector*]. *Library Journal* 98 (August 1973).

"Radar Screen." *New York Herald Tribune* (April 20, 1958).

Ratcliff, Carter. "New York" [review of exhibitions at Sidney Janis and Betty Parsons galleries]. *Art International* 14 (January 1970).

Redfern, John. "Smile-Styler to the Smart Set" [review of ICA exhibition]. *Daily Express* (London) (May 2, 1952).

Reed, Judith K. "The Art Book Library" [review of *All in Line*]. *Art Digest* (August 1, 1945).

Reichek, Jesse, ed. "Steinberg on the City: Part Two." *Journal of the American Institute of Planners* 27 (August 1961).

[Review of *Art of Living*]. *New York Herald Tribune* (October 7, 1949).

[Review of *The Labyrinth*]. *Manchester Guardian* (May 5, 1961).

[Review of *The Labyrinth*]. *New York Herald Tribune Lively Arts* (January 1, 1961).

[Review of *The Labyrinth*]. *Times Literary Supplement* (London) (August 4, 1961).

Rey, Stéphane. "Giacometti, Steinberg et le surréalisme." *Le Phare Dimanche* (Paris) (February 26, 1967).

Rivers, Larry. "Young Draftsman on Master Draftsmen." *Art News* 53 (January 1955).

Robels, Helga. "Saul Steinberg: Cat's Death." *Museen in Köln: Bulletin* 12, no. 6 (December 1967).

Roberts, Colette. "Exposition à New York." *Art d'Aujourd'hui* (Paris) 10 (January 1967).

R[obinson], A[my]. "Bookshelf" [review of *Art of Living*]. *Art News* 48 (November 1949).

Rogow, Lee. [Review of *The Passport*]. *Saturday Review of Literature* (December 4, 1954).

Rosenberg, Harold. "Saul Steinberg's Art World." *Art News* 65 (March 1966).

———. "Steinberg: A Unique Artist—a Specialist in the Riddles of Identity." *Vogue* (January 1, 1967).

———. "The Art World" [review of exhibitions at Sidney Janis and Betty Parsons galleries]. *The New Yorker* (March 17, 1973).

Rudikoff, Sonya. "Books" [review of *The Passport*]. *Arts Digest* (December 15, 1954).

Rudofsky, Bernard. "For the Honor of the Fleet; Murals for American Export Liners." *Interiors* 108 (December 1948).

Russell, John. "Vasari to Steinberg" [review of ICA exhibition]. *Sunday Times* (London) (May 11, 1952).

———. "Art: Steinberg's Lines on Life" [review]. *New York Times* (November 19, 1976).

Sadolin, Ebbe. "Saul Steinberg og København." *Berlingske Tidendes Kronik* (March 4, 1967).

"Satire by Steinberg." *Virginia Museum of Fine Arts: Members' Bulletin* (November 1953).

"Saul Steinberg in Europa—Kunst und Cartoons." *Artis* 9 (1968).

"Saul Steinberg" [exhibit plans]. *New York Times* (September 8, 1946).

"Saul Steinberg's Secret Underwear." *PM* (New York) (March 10, 1946).

Savary, Michèle. "Les Expositions à Paris: Saul Steinberg" [review of Galerie Maeght exhibition]. *Tribune de Genève* (April 30, 1953).

Sawyer, Kenneth B. "Art and Artists." *New York Herald Tribune* (Paris) (May 2, 1953).

Schaden, Herman. "An Artist Not-in-Residence." *Washington Star* (November 16, 1967).

Schmeller, Alfred. "Die smarte Welt als Dorotheum." *Kurier* (December 18, 1956).

Schneider, Pierre. "Steinberg at the Louvre: A Museum Tour." *Art in America* (July 1967).

———. "Les Vertiges de Steinberg." *L'Express* (Paris) (October 22–28, 1973).

Schonberg, Harold C. "Artist Behind the Steinbergian Mask." *New York Times Magazine* (November 13, 1966).

Schultz, Ben. "Parlor of a Satirist: A Series of Photographs." *Interiors* (New York) 110, no. 3 (October 1950).

Schuwer, Philippe. "Saul Steinberg ou le délire bien concerté." *Techniques Graphiques* 65 (September–October 1966).

Schwartz, E. "Paris" [review of Galerie Maeght exhibition]. *Art International* 15 (September 1971).

Shirey, David L. "Lord of the Line." *Newsweek* (December 12, 1966).

Simon, Karl G. "Die Strich-Dichter—Notizen zu einer Aesthetik des Trivialen." *Magnum* 48 (June 1963).

"Uno *Slide-Viewer* per diffondere una cartella d'arte." *Domus* 506 (January 1972).

Sosset, L. L. "Les Expositions à Bruxelles." *Les Beaux-Arts* (Brussels) (March 18, 1967).

Staats, Margaret, and Matthiesen, Lucas. "The Genetics of Art: Part II" [interviews with artists]. *Quest/77* (New York) (July–August 1977).

[Staber, Margit]. "Bilder als Autobiografie in Fortsetzungen" [interview]. *Tages Anzeiger Magazin* (November 20, 1971).

Stein, Ralph. [Review of *All in Line*]. *Saturday Review of Literature* (July 7, 1945).

"Steinberg." *Art News and Review* 4, no. 8 (May 17, 1952).

"Steinberg" [review of ICA exhibition]. *Architect and Building News* (London) (May 8, 1952).

"Steinberg at Brussels." *Newsweek* (April 28, 1958).

"Steinberg. One-Man Show at Museum of Modern Art, Brussels" [review]. *New York Times* (March 22, 1967).

"Steinberg at the Races." *Sports Illustrated* (November 11, 1963).

"Steinberg, Satirist." *Time* (April 26, 1943).

Steinberg, Saul. "Life in the Guatavir Line." *Life* (May 1940).

———. "Mottoes Illustrated." *Harper's* (August 1946).

———. "Furniture News from France." *Interiors* (New York) 106 (February 1947).

———. "Recapitulation." *Architectural Review* (London) 108 (December 1950).

———. "Italy; Drawings." *Harper's* (February 1952).

———. "Built in U.S.A.: Postwar architecture, 1945–52." *Art News* 51 (February 1953).

———. "Steinberg at the Bat." *Life* (July 11, 1955).

———. "Drawings of Athens." *Harper's* (February 1956).

———. "Steinberg, U.S.A." *Harper's* (September 1960).

———. "Statements and Documents." *Daedalus* 89, no. 1. (Winter 1960).

———. "The Nose Problem." *Location* (New York) 1, no. 1 (Spring 1963).

———. "Our False-Front Culture." *Look* (January 9, 1968).

"Steinberg and Society." *Newsweek* (February 11, 1952).

"Steinberg and Sterne." *Life* (August 27, 1951).

Stonier, G. W. "Steinberg." *New Statesman and Nation* 43 (May 24, 1952).

"Straight from the Hand and Mouth of Steinberg." *Life* (December 10, 1965).

Strelow, Hans. "Das Normale ist das Absurde: Saul Steinberg und seine Welt." *Frankfurter Allgemeine Zeitung* (January 10, 1970).

Stubbe, W. "Erwerbungen der graphischen Sammlung, Kunsthalle Hamburg in den Jahren 1968 und 1969." *Jahrbuch der Hamburger Kunstsammlungen*, 1969.

Taubman, Howard. "Americans Score U.S. Fair Exhibits." *New York Times* (April 24, 1958).

———. "Brussels: American Mistakes and Lessons." *New York Times Magazine* (June 6, 1958).

Taylor, Pamela. "Book List—Art of Living." *Saturday Review of Literature* (December 10, 1949).

Tenand, Suzanne. "Sous le ciel de Paris." *Tribune des Nations* (April 24, 1953).

Toffler, Alvin. "A Quantity of Culture." *Fortune* (November 1961).

Tolbert, Sergeant F. X. "What Does a Marine Look Like?" *Saturday Home Magazine* (1945).

Valsecchi, Marco. "Un Graffito di Steinberg in un portone a Milano." *Il Giorno* (Milan) (March 7, 1962).

Wahl, Kenneth. "Imagination and Fantasy." *The Birch Bark* (Birch Wathen School paper, New York) 46, no. 5 (April 1973).

Waldron, E. "Saul Steinberg." *Publishers Weekly* (May 7, 1973).

Warnod, Jeanine. "En 50 coups de tampon, Steinberg dénonce l'humanité enrégimentée." *Figaro* (June 18, 1971).

———. "Les Piges de Steinberg." *Figaro* (October 24, 1973).

Whitman, Alden. "Nabokov, near 71, Gets Gift for 70th." *New York Times* (March 18, 1970).

Willard, Charlotte. "Creator at Play." *New York Post* (December 3, 1966).

Williams, Monique. "Depuis qu'il est à Paris, Saul Steinberg, le plus grand des humoristes américains, est obsédé par l'obelisque." *L'Intransigeant* (Paris) (May 7, 1953).

Worth, Allan. [Review of *The Passport*]. *San Francisco Chronicle* (November 28, 1954).

Young, Vernon. "With Incisive, Satirical Pen, Steinberg Limns the Contemporary Scene." *Gentry* (Fall 1955).

Graphics

The text of this book was set in the film version of Janson, a replica of a typeface long thought to have been made by the Dutchman Anton Janson, who was a practicing type founder in Leipzig, Germany, during the years 1668–87. It has been conclusively demonstrated, however, that these types are actually the work of a Hungarian, Nicholas Kis (1650–1702), who probably learned his trade from the master Dutch type founder Dirk Voskens.

This book was photo-composed in film on the VIP by Typographic Images, Inc. The black and white reproduction was printed by The Murray Printing Co. The color separations were produced by Chanticleer Press, Inc. The color reproduction was printed by Rae Publishing Co., Inc. The book was bound by Economy Bookbinding Corporation.

Peter Mollman directed the production and manufacturing.
Lesley Krauss supervised the copy editing and proofreading.
R. D. Scudellari designed the book and directed the graphics.